DEADLY DISEASES AND EPIDEMICS

SARS

D0815937

Joaquima Serradell

CONSULTING EDITOR
The Late **I. Edward Alcamo**
Distinguished Teaching Professor of Microbiology,
SUNY Farmingdale

FOREWORD BY
David Heymann
World Health Organization

CHELSEA HOUSE
P U B L I S H E R S
A Haights Cross Communications ◆ Company ®
Philadelphia

COVER IMAGE: The SARS virus, a type of coronavirus, as seen through a transmission electron microscope.

Dedication

We dedicate the books in the DEADLY DISEASES AND EPIDEMICS series to Ed Alcamo, whose wit, charm, intelligence, and commitment to biology education were second to none.

CHELSEA HOUSE PUBLISHERS

VP, NEW PRODUCT DEVELOPMENT Sally Cheney
DIRECTOR OF PRODUCTION Kim Shinners
CREATIVE MANAGER Takeshi Takahashi
MANUFACTURING MANAGER Diann Grasse

Staff for SARS

EXECUTIVE EDITOR Tara Koellhoffer
ASSOCIATE EDITOR Beth Reger
EDITORIAL ASSISTANT Kuorkor Dzani
PRODUCTION EDITOR Noelle Nardone
PHOTO EDITOR Sarah Bloom
SERIES DESIGNER Terry Mallon
COVER DESIGNER Keith Trego
LAYOUT 21st Century Publishing and Communications, Inc.

A Haights Cross Communications ✦ Company ®

http://www.chelseahouse.com

First Printing

1 3 5 7 9 8 6 4 2

Library of Congress Cataloging-in-Publication Data

Serradell, Joaquima.
  SARS/Joaquima Serradell.
    p. cm.—(Deadly diseases and epidemics)
  Includes bibliographical references.
  ISBN 0-7910-8184-2 (hc)—ISBN 0-7910-8380-2 (pb)
  1. SARS (Disease) I. Title. II. Series.
RC776.S27S47 2005
616.2—dc22

                                                    2004029797

All links and web addresses were checked and verified to be correct at the time of publication. Because of the dynamic nature of the web, some addresses and links may have changed since publication and may no longer be valid.

Table of Contents

Foreword
David Heymann, World Health Organization   6

1.   A SARS Tale: Introduction   8

2.   SARS: A Global Epidemic   10

3.   SARS and Other Viral Infections   24

4.   SARS: Spread and Symptoms   40

5.   Diagnosis and Management of SARS   49

6.   Treatment of SARS   62

7.   Prevention and Public Health Measures   72

8.   Impact and Significance of SARS   80

Appendices   88

Glossary   97

Bibliography   101

Further Reading   106

Websites   107

Index   108

Foreword

In the 1960s, many of the infectious diseases that had terrorized generations were tamed. After a century of advances, the leading killers of Americans both young and old were being prevented with new vaccines or cured with new medicines. The risk of death from pneumonia, tuberculosis (TB), meningitis, influenza, whooping cough, and diphtheria declined dramatically. New vaccines lifted the fear that summer would bring polio, and a global campaign was on the verge of eradicating smallpox worldwide. New pesticides like DDT cleared mosquitoes from homes and fields, thus reducing the incidence of malaria, which was present in the southern United States and which remains a leading killer of children worldwide. New technologies produced safe drinking water and removed the risk of cholera and other water-borne diseases. Science seemed unstoppable. Disease seemed destined to all but disappear.

But the euphoria of the 1960s has evaporated.

The microbes fought back. Those causing diseases like TB and malaria evolved resistance to cheap and effective drugs. The mosquito developed the ability to defuse pesticides. New diseases emerged, including AIDS, Legionnaires, and Lyme disease. And diseases which had not been seen in decades re-emerged, as the hantavirus did in the Navajo Nation in 1993. Technology itself actually created new health risks. The global transportation network, for example, meant that diseases like West Nile virus could spread beyond isolated regions and quickly become global threats. Even modern public health protections sometimes failed, as they did in 1993 in Milwaukee, Wisconsin, resulting in 400,000 cases of the digestive system illness cryptosporidiosis. And, more recently, the threat from smallpox, a disease believed to be completely eradicated, has returned along with other potential bioterrorism weapons such as anthrax.

The lesson is that the fight against infectious diseases will never end.

In our constant struggle against disease, we as individuals have a weapon that does not require vaccines or drugs, and that is the warehouse of knowledge. We learn from the history of science that "modern" beliefs can be wrong. In this series of books, for example, you will learn that diseases like syphilis were once thought to be caused by eating potatoes. The invention of the microscope set science on the right path. There are more positive lessons from history. For example, smallpox was eliminated by vaccinating everyone who had come in contact with an infected person. This "ring" approach to smallpox control is still the preferred method for confronting an outbreak, should the disease be intentionally reintroduced.

At the same time, we are constantly adding new drugs, new vaccines, and new information to the warehouse. Recently, the entire human genome was decoded. So too was the genome of the parasite that causes malaria. Perhaps by looking at the microbe and the victim through the lens of genetics we will be able to discover new ways to fight malaria, which remains the leading killer of children in many countries.

Because of advances in our understanding of such diseases as AIDS, entire new classes of anti-retroviral drugs have been developed. But resistance to all these drugs has already been detected, so we know that AIDS drug development must continue.

Education, experimentation, and the discoveries that grow out of them are the best tools to protect health. Opening this book may put you on the path of discovery. I hope so, because new vaccines, new antibiotics, new technologies, and, most importantly, new scientists are needed now more than ever if we are to remain on the winning side of this struggle against microbes.

David Heymann
Executive Director
Communicable Diseases Section
World Health Organization
Geneva, Switzerland

1

A SARS Tale: Introduction

Wow, that was a close call! I didn't realize that my dad was in such danger, but now that I understand a little more about viruses and infections, it all makes perfect sense. I can't wait to tell my friends Pete and Tom about how my dad is a hero. Just think! A hero in my own family.

My name is Paul. I'm a junior in high school. It's not that I don't love my folks, but they aren't very exciting. Sometimes I wish I had famous or cooler parents. It's not really fair; my friend Patty's dad is a professional hockey player. We see his picture in the newspaper all the time and she has great stories about all the celebrities he meets. Brian's mom is the mayor of our town; Roger's older brother is the quarterback of the Naval Academy football team. And my family? Well, my dad sells paper clips— not a particularly glamorous career. Dad certainly never had his picture in the newspaper—at least not until last week.

Something happened last week that changed our lives. Dad was on a flight to Singapore, where he buys many of the paperclip products he sells. He noticed that several of the other passengers had really bad coughs. Ordinarily, he wouldn't even have given that fact a second thought, but earlier, during the same flight, he had read an article about SARS (severe acute respiratory syndrome), and all the coughing had made him a little worried.

He mentioned his concerns to the flight attendant, who said that it was nothing to worry about—people cough on every flight. She suggested that my dad just relax. But Dad wasn't satisfied with that response. He walked around and wrote down the seat numbers of the people who were coughing, along with a brief physical description of each person. After the plane landed, Dad gave his information to the health officers at the immigration office. They treated him politely, but they probably thought he was a little crazy for being so concerned about a few people coughing.

It turned out that Dad had been right for worrying. The very next day, one of the coughers from the airplane went to the emergency room at the hospital in Singapore with a high fever, chills, and difficulty breathing. He was diagnosed as having SARS and was immediately isolated in the **quarantine** ward, so he would not infect anyone else. The authorities asked him to name all the people with whom he had been in close contact over the last few days, but that was impossible. He didn't know the names of any of the 204 other passengers from the flight he'd been on the day before. Luckily, a health officer at the airport immigration office remembered the man—my dad—who had come in with the list of coughing passengers. They found the list, rounded up the eight passengers, and isolated them all until they were no longer contagious.

Dad had stopped a serious SARS **outbreak** from happening. It could have affected up to 100,000 people in the country and caused as many as 15,000 deaths. The prime minister of Singapore gave my dad a medal of honor in a public ceremony of thanks. Dad was also featured on the cover of *TIME* magazine and on the front page of our local newspaper, *The Guardian*.

Now, the phone doesn't stop ringing. Reporters want to interview Dad, and they even try to speak with me to get my thoughts about having such a thoughtful and clever father.

After my dad's amazing experience, I listen to him when he gives advice about paying attention to what's going on around me! Being observant helped my dad prevent a dangerous disease from spreading and may have saved a lot of lives.

2

SARS: A Global Epidemic

The significance of SARS as a public health threat is considerable. All new infectious diseases are poorly understood (by definition) as they emerge and are often associated with high mortality rates. SARS was no exception, and proved to be an especially difficult disease to diagnose and treat. Many new diseases have features that limit their potential for international spread. Some never establish efficient person-to-person transmission. Others depend on the presence of a mosquito or other vector as part of the transmission cycle. Still others remain closely tied to a specific geographical region or ecosystem. For some, patients are visibly too ill to travel during the most infectious period. In contrast, SARS passed readily from person to person, required no vector, had no particular geographic affinity, mimicked the symptoms of many other diseases, took its heaviest toll on hospital staff, killed around 11% of those infected, and spread internationally with alarming ease.

—Secretariat's report to the
World Health Organization's Executive Board,
January 2004

THE PANIC BEGINS

In February 2003, a 48-year-old Chinese-American businessman named Johnny Cheng checked into the French Hospital in Hanoi, Vietnam. Three days before he got sick, he had arrived on a plane from Hong Kong, where he had stayed at the Metropole Hotel during his business trip. Now, he lay deathly ill in the hospital, where his condition baffled the doctors who examined him.

Cheng was showing symptoms of severe pneumonia. According to one nurse who treated him, "he was coughing a lot and developing a great amount of phlegm. In fact, he was coughing all night. . . ." But Cheng also showed other symptoms that did not indicate pneumonia: He had shortness of breath and a high fever in addition to his cough, which led doctors to believe he was suffering from a more unusual disease.

Hoping for help in identifying the mysterious illness, the doctors called in infectious disease specialist Dr. Carlo Urbani, who worked for the World Health Organization (WHO). Urbani arrived at the French Hospital on February 26, and began a weeklong observation of Cheng's condition, during which he studied the man's symptoms and collected blood and saliva samples for analysis. Despite Urbani's work and the efforts of the hospital staff to save Cheng, relatives removed Cheng from the hospital and brought him back to Hong Kong, where he later died. Urbani, however, had succeeded in recognizing that he and his fellow medical experts were dealing with a new disease—not pneumonia. It got its own name—severe acute respiratory syndrome (or SARS) on March 15. By then, however, a great deal of damage had already been done.

On March 11, while flying to Bangkok, Thailand, to attend a conference, Dr. Urbani began to feel ill, and realized he was suffering from the same disease he had been observing in Johnny Cheng. Urbani moved quickly to isolate himself in a hospital to try to protect others from the disease. Over a period of several days, his condition grew worse, and his respiratory system collapsed. Ultimately, Urbani died of the very disease he had first identified and named.

Meanwhile, the new disease was continuing to spread—and to claim more lives (Figure 2.1). Five other medical workers at the French Hospital where Cheng had been treated died of SARS. Altogether, 62 cases in Vietnam were traced to Johnny Cheng. Cases also began to appear in people in Hong Kong, particularly those who had stayed at the Metropole Hotel

(continued on page 14)

11

DR. CARLO URBANI

Dr. Carlo Urbani, an epidemiologist and expert on **communicable diseases**, died of severe acute respiratory syndrome (SARS). Dr. Urbani worked in public health programs in Cambodia, Laos, and Vietnam, but was based in Hanoi, Vietnam.

Dr. Carlo Urbani was the first World Health Organization (WHO) officer to identify the outbreak of SARS, in the Chinese-American businessman who had been admitted to a small hospital in Hanoi. The patient had an unusual, influenza-like virus. Hospital officials in Hanoi asked whether someone from the WHO would examine the patient. Dr. Urbani answered that call. He suspected that the small hospital was facing something unusual. Dr. Urbani chose to work in the hospital, documenting findings, arranging for samples to be sent for testing and reinforcing infection control. The hospital established an isolation ward that was kept under guard. Dr. Urbani worked directly with the medical staff of the hospital to strengthen morale and to keep fear in check as SARS revealed itself to be highly contagious and **virulent**. Of the first 60 patients who became infected with SARS, more than half were health-care workers. To protect their families and community, some health-care workers put themselves at great personal risk, deciding to sleep in the hospital, effectively sealing themselves off from the outside world.

Urbani did not survive to see the successes resulting from his early detection of SARS. On March 11, 2003, he began to have symptoms of the disease during a flight to Bangkok. On his arrival, he told his colleague from the Centers for Disease Control and Prevention (CDC) who greeted him at the airport not to approach him. They sat down at a distance from each other in silence, waiting for an ambulance to bring protective gear. Urbani fought SARS for the next 18 days in an isolation room in a Bangkok hospital. He died on March 29, 2003. Dr. Carlo Urbani was 46. He was married and the father of three children.

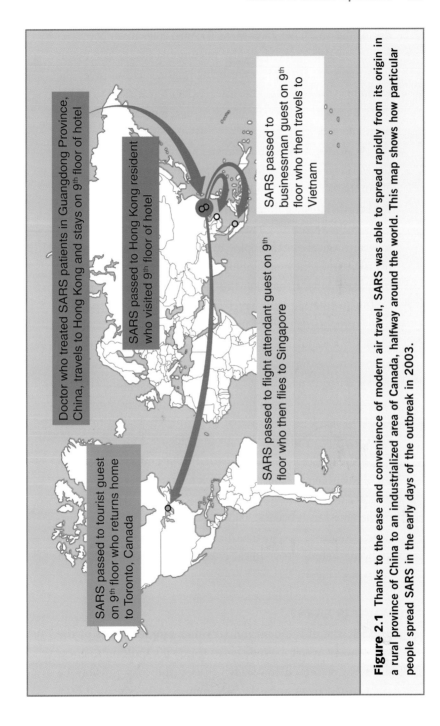

Doctor who treated SARS patients in Guangdong Province, China, travels to Hong Kong and stays on 9th floor of hotel

SARS passed to Hong Kong resident who visited 9th floor of hotel

SARS passed to businessman guest on 9th floor who then travels to Vietnam

SARS passed to flight attendant guest on 9th floor who then flies to Singapore

SARS passed to tourist guest on 9th floor who returns home to Toronto, Canada

Figure 2.1 Thanks to the ease and convenience of modern air travel, SARS was able to spread rapidly from its origin in a rural province of China to an industrialized area of Canada, halfway around the world. This map shows how particular people spread SARS in the early days of the outbreak in 2003.

(continued from page 11)

during the time Cheng was there. By April 2003, many countries were reporting cases of similar pneumonia-like viral illnesses in patients, and people were being quarantined all over the world to avoid spreading the disease (Figure 2.2). By December 2003, a total of 774 people had died, and more than 8,000 had been infected.

As word got out about the potentially deadly new disease, the world was seized with panic. Headlines screamed warnings about the "Killer Bug," and people took personal precautions to fend off the dreaded illness. Throughout Asia and even in other parts of the world that had fewer cases of SARS, people began to wear surgical masks, hoping to avoid contaminated droplets from the air or the breath of other people. Some people refused to shake hands, afraid that the disease could be transmitted by touch. International travel slowed dramatically, especially to areas reporting cases of the disease. Toronto, Canada, which is usually a popular vacation spot for tourists from the United States, saw a 90% decline in its hotel and restaurant business after seven local people died and hundreds were quarantined in response to the SARS outbreak. Business conferences and even sporting events were canceled as people chose not to travel abroad if they could possibly avoid it (Figure 2.3).

Although the response of the media and general public may have been extreme, it is easy to understand the terrible fear that this deadly new viral disease caused. After the first reports of the illness in February 2003, SARS spread to more than two dozen countries in North America, South America, Europe, and Asia before the medical community was finally able to contain it (Figure 2.4).

WHAT IS SARS?

SARS is one of the new and very dangerous diseases of the 21st century, which include avian (bird) flu and Ebola. These diseases are caused by deadly viruses and may possibly be transmitted from animals to humans. SARS is caused by a

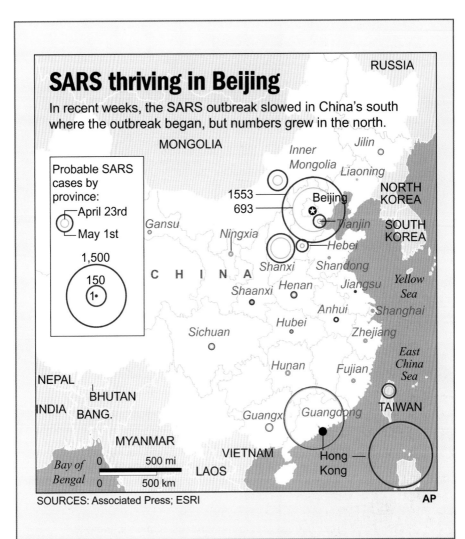

SARS thriving in Beijing

In recent weeks, the SARS outbreak slowed in China's south where the outbreak began, but numbers grew in the north.

Probable SARS cases by province:
April 23rd
May 1st

1,500
150
1.

1553
693

Beijing
Tianjin
Hebei

RUSSIA
MONGOLIA
Inner Mongolia
Jilin
Liaoning
NORTH KOREA
SOUTH KOREA
Gansu
Ningxia
Shanxi
Shandong
Yellow Sea
C H I N A
Shaanxi
Henan
Jiangsu
Anhui
Shanghai
Hubei
Zhejiang
Sichuan
East China Sea
Hunan
Fujian
NEPAL
BHUTAN
INDIA BANG.
Guangx
Guangdong
TAIWAN
MYANMAR
VIETNAM
Hong Kong
Bay of Bengal
500 mi
500 km
LAOS
0
0

SOURCES: Associated Press; ESRI   AP

Figure 2.2 Although the first cases of SARS appeared in November 2002 and were limited to a small part of the Quangdong province, by April 2003, the new and mysterious disease had spread widely throughout China, and had even been found in the capital city of Beijing. This map from the Associated Press, published during the SARS outbreak in the spring of 2003, shows the locations and numbers of SARS cases in various areas of China.

Figure 2.3 The outbreak of SARS in China and other parts of Asia caused many people around the world to abandon their travel plans to those areas, even before the World Health Organization issued its travel advisories suggesting that nonessential travel be avoided. Because of this dramatic decrease in travel to Asia, China and other nations took a tremendous economic blow, particularly in the tourism industry. This photograph of a Chinese temple shows how places that were once filled with tourists were left virtually abandoned during the SARS epidemic.

special kind of **virus** called a coronavirus (see Chapter 3 for more details). It is very **infectious**—which means it is easily spread from one person to another. The virus remains active and is able to cause infection in both urine and feces for 24

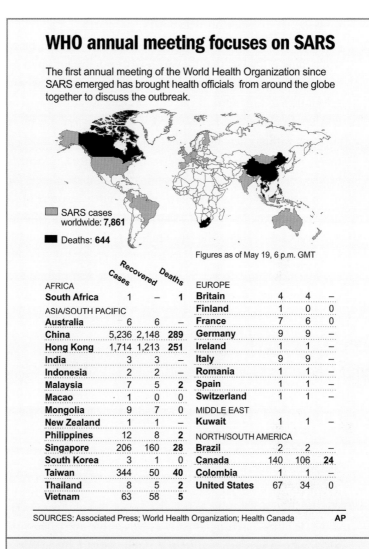

WHO annual meeting focuses on SARS

The first annual meeting of the World Health Organization since SARS emerged has brought health officials from around the globe together to discuss the outbreak.

SARS cases worldwide: **7,861**

Deaths: **644**

Figures as of May 19, 6 p.m. GMT

	Cases	Recovered	Deaths
AFRICA			
South Africa	1	–	1
ASIA/SOUTH PACIFIC			
Australia	6	6	–
China	5,236	2,148	289
Hong Kong	1,714	1,213	251
India	3	3	–
Indonesia	2	2	–
Malaysia	7	5	2
Macao	1	0	0
Mongolia	9	7	0
New Zealand	1	1	–
Philippines	12	8	2
Singapore	206	160	28
South Korea	3	1	0
Taiwan	344	50	40
Thailand	8	5	2
Vietnam	63	58	5

	Cases	Recovered	Deaths
EUROPE			
Britain	4	4	–
Finland	1	0	0
France	7	6	0
Germany	9	9	–
Ireland	1	1	–
Italy	9	9	–
Romania	1	1	–
Spain	1	1	–
Switzerland	1	1	–
MIDDLE EAST			
Kuwait	1	1	–
NORTH/SOUTH AMERICA			
Brazil	2	2	–
Canada	140	106	24
Colombia	1	1	–
United States	67	34	0

SOURCES: Associated Press; World Health Organization; Health Canada   **AP**

Figure 2.4 Thanks to the coordinated efforts of both national and international health agencies, the SARS epidemic was contained before it could spread far enough to infect or kill massive numbers of people. At the first meeting of the World Health Organization after the SARS outbreak began, which took place in May 2003, WHO officials published the numbers of people who caught SARS and the number who died from it. Those figures were used to create this map, showing the location and numbers of SARS cases around the world.

to 48 hours. If a person with SARS has diarrhea, his or her stool can harbor active viruses for up to 4 days! Even more frightening is the fact that the SARS virus can live for up to 24 hours without being inside a **host** (a person or animal whose cells it uses to function). It can contaminate surfaces—such as doorknobs or light switches—and if someone touches these surfaces within a few hours after an infected person touched them, he or she will risk contracting the virus. Scientists believe the virus's ability to contaminate inanimate objects for up to a full day explains in part why the virus was spread so quickly by people who flew in airplanes after the initial outbreak. Besides riding in an enclosed flight cabin with infected people, where air is continually recirculated, it might have been possible to get SARS by touching a contaminated meal tray or bathroom door.

THE ORIGINS AND SPREAD OF SARS

Scientists believe the SARS virus first cropped up in the Guangdong province, an agricultural area of southwestern China, where 80 million people live and work mainly as farmers. Many local residents practice traditional farming methods that keep them in close contact with animals such as chicken, ducks, fish, and pigs—all of which have been known to spread disease to humans. Although the rest of the world only learned about SARS between February and March 2003, towns in Guangdong had already recorded several cases of the mysterious new illness, starting as early as November 2002. The first SARS patient was believed to be a public servant living in the town of Foshan. Fortunately for him, he survived his battle with SARS, but he nonetheless managed to pass the disease on to at least four other people.

The earliest cases showed up as highly contagious and severe **atypical pneumonia**, and seemed to be affecting mainly health-care workers and the members of their households. Many of the cases were rapidly fatal.

A doctor from Guangzhou, who had been treating some of the patients with the illness, may have been the one to spread SARS beyond Guangdong province when he traveled to Hong Kong to attend a wedding. After he checked into the Metropole Hotel (the same place where businessman Johnny Cheng was staying), nine other guests were hospitalized with the symptoms of what later became known as SARS.

The Chinese government has long been known for trying to conceal bad news, even from its own people, so it was not surprising that officials worked hard to prevent word of the initial November outbreak from spreading in order to avoid causing a public panic and a possible economic crisis. Because of the delay in reporting the cases, however, people continued to travel normally and health workers did not always take the proper precautions to avoid becoming infected themselves. As a result, **clusters** of SARS cases began to pop up around the globe. By the end of March 2003, Hong Kong had seen a total of 320 cases over a period of under three weeks. Then, as infected people (particularly those who had been guests at the Metropole Hotel) resumed their travels, the disease was carried to Vietnam, Singapore, and Toronto, Canada.

In Vietnam, the outbreak was traced back to a man who was admitted to a hospital in Hanoi with high fever, dry cough, and mild sore throat. Following his admission, approximately 20 members of the hospital staff became sick with similar symptoms.

In Singapore, health authorities reported three cases of atypical pneumonia, one of which was a female flight attendant who had stayed at the Metropole Hotel. More than 100 SARS cases in Singapore were ultimately traced back to this one woman.

Canadian health authorities informed international health agencies of a cluster of patients from a single hospital in Toronto. The disease came to Toronto with travelers who had flown in from Singapore.

Once the disease began to reach **epidemic** proportions, the Chinese were forced to admit, partly in response to pressure from the WHO, that there had been earlier cases in Guangdong. By March 2003, the WHO issued a global alert about cases of severe atypical pneumonia following mounting reports of cases among staff in certain Hanoi and Hong Kong hospitals. The health alert included a rare emergency travel advisory (Figure 2.5) to international travelers, medical professionals, and health authorities, instructing all individuals traveling to affected areas to be watchful for the development of symptoms—including fever, headache, muscle stiffness, diarrhea, shortness of breath, and a dry cough—for a period of 10 days after their return.

THE WORLD HEALTH ORGANIZATION

The World Health Organization (WHO) is an international association established in 1948 with the goal of improving human health. WHO helps countries strengthen their health services, provides assistance in health emergencies, promotes disease prevention and control, and works to set international food safety, medical, and health standards.

According to the WHO's constitution, *health* is defined as a state of complete physical, mental, and social well-being—not merely the absence of disease or infirmity, which had been the way health was described for centuries before the WHO was founded.

The WHO is headquartered in Geneva, Switzerland, and governed by its 192 member states through the World Health Assembly. The main task of the World Health Assembly is to approve the WHO program and the budget and to decide policy questions.

In addition to its Geneva headquarters, the WHO has offices in most countries of the world, including six regional offices:

- Regional Office for Africa—located in Brazzaville, Republic of Congo

According to the WHO, by August 2003, SARS had infected more than 8,422 people worldwide, and of these, 908 had died. In the United States, only eight people were confirmed to have been in contact with the SARS virus. All eight had traveled to other parts of the world where SARS had been spreading, but the people had not carried the illness to communities in the United States, a fact that is not yet fully understood. Heightened vigilance, control measures, and preparedness that followed the WHO's global alerts are thought to have contributed to the prevention of further significant outbreaks, and likely prevented what could have been a worldwide disaster that might have killed many thousands of people.

- **Regional Office for Europe—located in Copenhagen, Denmark**

- **Regional Office for Southeast Asia—located in New Delhi, India**

- **Regional Office for the Americas/Pan American Health Organization—located in Washington, D.C.**

- **Regional Office for the Eastern Mediterranean—located in Cairo, Egypt**

- **Regional Office for the Western Pacific—located in Manila, Philippines.**

The WHO is probably best known for its successful campaign to eliminate the deadly disease smallpox, which had killed and maimed millions throughout history. By undertaking an intensive campaign to vaccinate people all over the world during the 1960s and 1970s, the WHO was able to eradicate smallpox as a naturally occurring disease. The last natural case of smallpox occurred in 1977. Today, smallpox exists only in scientific laboratories.

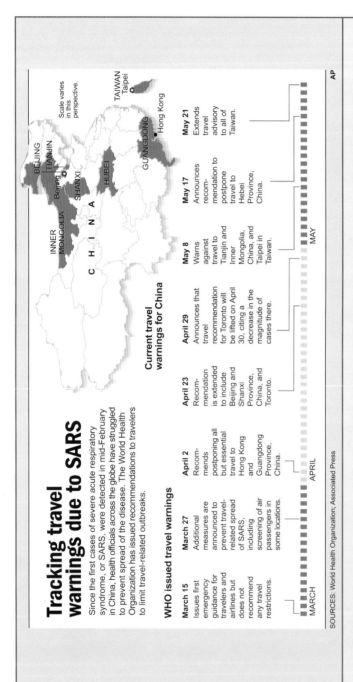

Tracking travel warnings due to SARS

Since the first cases of severe acute respiratory syndrome, or SARS, were detected in mid-February in China, health officials across the globe have struggled to prevent spread of the disease. The World Health Organization has issued recommendations to travelers to limit travel-related outbreaks.

WHO issued travel warnings

March 15
Issues first emergency guidance for travelers and airlines but does not recommend any travel restrictions.

March 27
Additional measures are announced to prevent travel-related spread of SARS, including screening of air passengers in some locations.

April 2
Recommends postponing all but essential travel to Hong Kong and Guangdong Province, China.

Current travel warnings for China

April 23
Recommendation is extended to include Beijing and Shanxi Province, China, and Toronto.

April 29
Announces that travel recommendation for Toronto will be lifted on April 30, citing a decrease in the magnitude of cases there.

May 8
Warns against travel to Tianjin and Inner Mongolia, China, and Taipei in Taiwan.

May 17
Announces recommendation to postpone travel to Hebei Province, China.

May 21
Extends travel advisory to all of Taiwan.

MARCH   APRIL   MAY

SOURCES: World Health Organization; Associated Press

AP

Figure 2.5 One of the most important strategies for stopping the spread of the SARS epidemic was the WHO's policy of issuing travel advisories regarding areas where SARS had been found. This illustration shows the areas of Asia affected by the WHO travel advisories, and the dates on which the advisories were issued for each place.

THE DEATH TOLL

Mortality (the number of people in a given population who die from an illness, in this case, SARS) was initially believed to be around 3%, but may, in fact, be as high as 15%. The WHO estimates that the **case fatality rate** (the number of deaths from a certain disease within a given period of time) for SARS ranges from 0% to 50%. The older the age group, the higher the fatality rate. In general, children experience a mild form of the disease with an extremely low death rate. Mortality rates are highest among the elderly and people who have weakened immune systems or are already struggling with other diseases. Elderly people are more likely to die from a SARS infection because they have reduced lung function that comes with age, as well as less efficient immune systems.

HOW SARS WAS CONTAINED

Measures to contain SARS (prevent it from spreading) took two major forms: **isolation** of symptomatic cases (people who showed obvious symptoms of the disease) to prevent transmission, and quarantine (the close observation of **asymptomatic** contacts—people who did not show symptoms but might have been infected—so that they could be isolated immediately if they did begin to show signs of the disease). Along with travel restrictions and advisories, the close watch kept on SARS patients was responsible to a large extent for stopping the further spread of the disease.

The terrifyingly rapid spread of a new and previously unidentified—and incurable—virus made the global medical community realize that, despite great advances in preventing and treating illness over the last century, the threat of infectious disease has not gone away. SARS has made all of us aware that deadly **pathogens** (disease-causing organisms) still exist and that it will take the cooperation of the entire world to stop them from killing huge numbers of people.

3

SARS and Other Viral Infections

An international team of scientists say they have conclusively identified the virus responsible for SARS. As suspected since the height of the outbreak, a coronavirus is behind the disease.

—CBC News (Canada), July 23, 2003

Infection is defined as a disease resulting from the presence of certain **microorganisms** (living things that are too small to be seen without a microscope) in the body. These organisms (commonly called "germs") can be single-celled amoebas, bacteria, or tiny viruses. Usually, they enter our bodies through our mouth and nose when we breathe, eat contaminated foods, or come into close contact with an infected person. They can also enter through the eyes or be transmitted sexually. Microorganisms can also get inside our bodies through cuts or open wounds.

GERM THEORY AND DISEASE

In the late 19th century, scientists came up with the **germ theory** of disease. It states that many diseases are caused by microorganisms and that microorganisms grow through reproduction rather than being spontaneously generated. This new understanding helped scientists see how infectious microorganisms could cause disease in humans. Now, they just had to find and isolate the specific organisms that caused particular diseases to have a better idea of how the illness might be treated or prevented.

In identifying agents that cause human disease, Robert Koch (1843–1910), a German country doctor, came up with a method by which an organism could be isolated from (taken out of) a sick animal or person, grown in the laboratory, and then used to infect a healthy individual who would develop the same disease and carry the same organism. Using this method, Koch helped scientists understand the nature of infectious diseases, and the ways in which they were transmitted between people and between animals and people. Koch's most influential contributions to medicine were the isolation of the tubercule

LOUIS PASTEUR

Louis Pasteur was born in 1822 in Dole, France. He was trained as a research chemist and became so well known and respected that, in 1854, at age 32, he became dean of the Faculty of Science at the University of Lille. At this time, Lille was the center of alcohol manufacturing in France.

A local industrialist asked Pasteur to look at his beer factory, where many of his vats of fermented beer were turning sour. After using a microscope to analyze samples from the vats, Pasteur found thousands of microorganisms. He was convinced that they were responsible for the beer going sour. Pasteur believed that they were the cause, rather than the result, of the putrid beer. Pasteur went on to study wine and milk as well as beer.

In 1865, he was asked to investigate his first disease, called *pebrine*, which affected the silkworm industry. Pasteur discovered that the disease was caused by a living organism, and he now become convinced that microbes could affect humans as well as beer, milk, and worms.

In this sense, Pasteur believed that microbes could spread diseases among humans. He developed his work by finding out ways humans could avoid getting diseases. He knew about the work done by Edward Jenner in inoculating people against smallpox. Pasteur reasoned that if a vaccine could be found for smallpox, then a vaccine could likely be found for all diseases.

In 1880, he found a vaccine by chance. His assistant, Chamberland, had inoculated some chickens with chicken cholera germs from an old culture that had been around for some time. The chickens did not die. Pasteur asked Chamberland to repeat what he had done but with a fresh culture of chicken cholera germs. Pasteur reasoned that a new culture would provide more potent germs. Two groups of chickens were inoculated; one group was given the old culture and another was not. Those chickens that had been inoculated with the old culture survived, and those that had not died. The chickens that had been inoculated with the old culture had become immune to chicken cholera.

In addition, Pasteur and his team studied the disease rabies. Most human victims of rabies died a painful death. Although the team could not identify the germ that caused rabies, they did learn that the rabies germ attacked the nervous system only after it had made its way to the brain. The team then traced the germ to the brain and spinal cord of infected animals and, by using dried spinal cords, they produced a vaccine for rabies.

Louis Pasteur's name is forever cemented in the history of medicine because he showed that microbes were the cause of disease and because his work helped lead to the development of many useful vaccines.

bacillus (the cause of tuberculosis) and the establishment of the essential steps (known as "Koch's Postulates;" see Box below) required to prove that an organism is the cause of disease.

KOCH'S POSTULATES

German bacteriologist Robert Koch came up with four steps that must be taken in determining the cause of disease. These have come to be known as "Koch's Postulates." They say:

1. **The pathogen must be found in all cases of the disease.** Scientists must carefully obtain samples from all suspected patients and find the same disease-causing organism present in each, if that organism is expected to be the reason for the illness.

2. **It must be isolated from the host and grown in pure culture.** The scientist must then take the pathogen and grow some of it in a laboratory, in order to have a fresh sample before going on to the next step.

3. **It must reproduce the original disease when introduced into a susceptible host.** The scientist must use the sample grown in the lab and place it (through injection, most often) into the body of a person or animal who is not immune to the disease in question. Only if the subject becomes ill with the disease can the pathogen be the cause.

4. **It must be found in the experimental host that was infected.** That is, the scientist must then take blood or other samples from the person or animal into whom the pathogen was introduced and confirm that the original pathogen is, indeed, present, and that it is not some other organism that is causing the disease.

WHAT IS A VIRUS?

A virus is a very small infectious organism—much smaller than a bacterium, another common disease-causing microorganism. Also unlike bacteria, viruses need a living cell in order to reproduce. In fact, some scientists do not even consider viruses to be living things. Because they are so small, they have very few components, and must be precisely packaged. A typical virus consists of genetic material surrounded by a protein coat, or **capsid**. Viruses contain nucleic acid, which can be made up of **RNA (ribonucleic acid)** or **DNA (deoxyribonucleic acid)** or both, and may be single- or double-stranded, and either circular or linear (Figure 3.1).

The virus's goal is to find a place where it can set up a "home" for itself and make many copies of its own genetic material. This is the virus's sole reason for existence. To achieve this goal, the virus invades the body of a living creature and attaches to one of its cells, which is then called the host cell. Once inside a cell, the virus releases its DNA or RNA, which contains the information needed to create new virus particles. By doing this, the virus essentially takes over the cell's usual function and forces it to make more virus particles instead of doing its regular job. At this point, the cell is said to be infected by the virus.

What ultimately happens to the invaded cell depends on the type of virus that attacks it. Some viruses kill the cells they infect. Others just alter the cell's function so that the cell loses control over its normal process of cell division. Some viruses incorporate a part or all of their genetic information into the host cell's DNA. Once inside the cell, the virus uses the cell's machinery to **replicate** (multiply) while putting regular cellular processes on hold.

VIRUSES AND HOSTS

Most viruses have a certain kind of host they prefer to live in. Some, such as the influenza virus, can infect humans and a variety of other animals. Most viruses that are commonly

Membrane glycoproteins

Spikes

Envelope

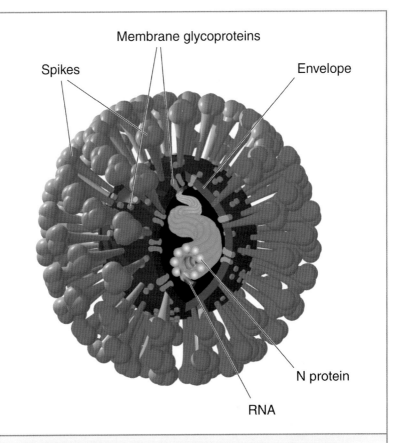

N protein

RNA

Figure 3.1 Viruses are tiny particles made up of little more than genetic material and a protein coat (like the virus illustrated here). Although they contain nucleic acids—either RNA or DNA—which all living cells need to reproduce, many scientists argue that viruses are not living things at all. This is because a virus cannot reproduce on its own. To multiply, it essentially has to "hijack" a host cell and use the cell's machinery to make new virus particles.

found in people, however, are spread from person to person, not from animals to people. Other viruses, such as the rabies virus or encephalitis viruses, infect animals primarily and humans only occasionally. Viruses are referred to as intracellular parasites. That is, they need a specific type of live host to allow them to produce energy and replicate. Without a proper host, they can't survive for long, if at all.

HOW VIRUSES CAUSE INFECTION

There are three requirements that must be met if a virus is going to successfully cause an infection. First, there must be enough of the virus present to cause infection. Different viruses need to be present in different amounts to infect a host. Second, the host cells must be susceptible to the virus. This means that the host must not be immune to the virus, like someone who has received a vaccination to prevent a certain disease would be. Finally, the host's local defenses must be absent when the virus attacks.

The body has a number of specific and nonspecific defenses against viruses and other pathogens. Physical barriers such as the skin and mucous membranes discourage easy entry into the body. Infected cells also make interferon, a special type of protein that can make non-infected cells more resistant to infection by many viruses. However, if a virus does enter the body, various types of white cells, such as lymphocytes, are able to attack and destroy infected cells. The outcome of virus infection varies depending on the virus. In some cases, there is little impact on the cell, and in other cases, the cell dies.

THE HUMAN IMMUNE SYSTEM

The human body is designed to help protect us against disease. It has several different ways to do this.

The body's first line of defense consists of physical barriers that act to keep pathogens (like viruses) from getting inside the cells. Among these barriers are the skin, the mucous membranes (which can trap pathogens in sticky mucus and expel them from the body), and cilia (hair-like structures in the nose, lungs, and other organs that help sweep foreign substances out of the body). Before it can mount a successful infection, the SARS virus must get past these physical defenses. Because it is carried in the breath of infected people, a person can breathe in the virus in the form of vapor, and it is carried to the lungs, where it can start an infection. It may also be able to get into the body through cuts or open wounds on the skin.

Once a foreign organism gets inside the body, the immune system launches another set of defense mechanisms. The immune system is made up of many different kinds of cells that play very special roles in destroying invaders and helping the body repair itself from damage done by infectious organisms. Among the immune cells that attack first are macrophages— large cells that literally gobble up invading organisms and kill them. (*Macro* refers to the large part of a cell, while *phage* means "eater of.")

But macrophages cannot eliminate an invader entirely on their own. So, the immune system also has white blood cells, or lymphocytes, that help stop an infection.

B cells, one type of lymphocyte, travel through the bloodstream, looking for foreign organisms. When they encounter cells they do not recognize, they attach to them and produce antibodies—proteins that will remain in the body and help it to recognize a particular pathogen quickly in the event of a future attack.

Meanwhile, T cells, another type of lymphocyte, also take part in the immune defense. There are two types of T cells. Regular, or helper, T cells locate invading pathogens and send out chemical signals to the rest of the body to let the immune system know an invasion is taking place. Killer T cells, on the other hand, not only recognize invaders, but also have the ability to attach to and destroy unfamiliar cells—whether these cells are viruses, bacteria, or even cancerous cells of the body's own tissues.

Together, these immune system cells are very good at keeping the body healthy, but they can be outnumbered when enough viruses or other pathogens enter and begin to infect the cells. Once an infection begins, it can take the immune system a long time, from days to weeks or even months, to completely destroy the invaders and end the infection. The faster an infection takes hold, the more dangerous it can be. And the SARS virus often infects with lightning speed.

TYPES OF VIRUSES

There are four main types of viruses, three of which are illustrated in Figure 3.2:

- **Icosahedral:** This kind of virus has an outer shell (capsid) made from 20 flat sides, which gives the virus a spherical shape. Most viruses are icosahedral.

- **Helical:** This type of virus has a capsid that is shaped like a rod.

- **Enveloped:** In these viruses, the capsid is encased in a baggy membrane, which can change shape but often looks spherical.

- **Complex:** A complex virus has its genetic material coated, but does not have a capsid.

Among the enveloped type of viruses is the **coronavirus**, which is responsible for SARS. The first known coronavirus was isolated from chickens in 1937.

SARS: A CORONAVIRUS

Severe acute respiratory syndrome (SARS) is caused by a previously unknown coronavirus, now called SARS-associated coronavirus (SARS-CoV).

Coronaviruses get their name because of the way they look: They appear to have a halo or crown (*corona* in Latin) when viewed under a microscope (Figure 3.3). Coronavirus particles are irregularly shaped with an outer envelope that

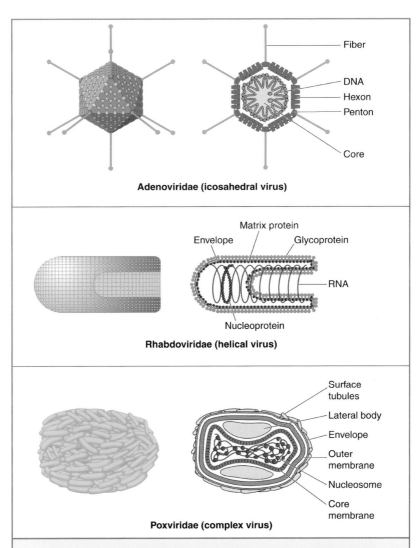

Figure 3.2 This diagram illustrates three of the four major kinds of viruses. At the top is an icosahedral virus, which is named for its characteristic 20-sided shape. At the center is a helical virus, named for its rod-like shape. At the bottom is a complex virus, which characteristically has coated genetic material, but does not have a capsid. The virus that causes SARS comes from the fourth category of viruses, not seen here—enveloped viruses, which get their name because their capsid is enclosed (or enveloped) in a baggy membrane.

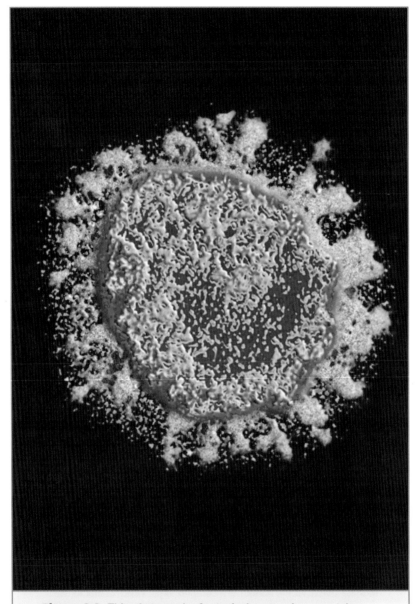

Figure 3.3 This photograph of a typical coronavirus was taken through an electron microscope. With the extraordinary detail the magnification produces, it is easy to see the "halo" that surrounds the virus, and the stubby peplomers that protrude from its surface.

has distinctive, "club-shaped" **peplomers** (a subunit of a virus particle). Coronaviruses are RNA (ribonucleic acid) viruses that replicate in the cytoplasm of the animal host cells, and cause disease in humans and animals, including the common cold. Coronavirus infections are very common and occur worldwide. The **incidence** of infection is strongly seasonal, with its greatest incidence among children in winter. Adult infections are less frequent. Coronaviruses can occasionally cause more severe disease, such as pneumonia, but this is rare. In fact, before SARS was discovered, the human coronaviruses previously known were only associated with mild diseases. SARS-related CoV seems to be the first coronavirus that regularly causes potentially fatal illness in humans.

The SARS virus is very hardy and can survive in the environment without being inside a host for several hours. All viruses have short lives when not attached to a living cell.

The new SARS coronavirus has some unusual properties. For one, the SARS virus can be grown in Vero cells (a cell line isolated in 1962 from a primate). This is an unusual characteristic of **HCoVs** (**human coronaviruses**), most of which cannot be cultivated. You might wonder, if coronaviruses usually cause only mild illness in humans, then how can this new coronavirus be responsible for a potentially life-threatening disease like SARS? Because the SARS virus is so recently identified, there is not yet enough information about it to determine the full range of illnesses that it might be able to cause. Coronaviruses have occasionally been linked to pneumonia in humans, especially in people with weakened immune systems. The viruses can also cause severe disease in animals.

The outbreak in China in the Guangdong province is believed to have started when humans became infected as they raised and slaughtered wild animals for food. Coronaviruses that are 99% similar genetically to the surface spike protein of

Figure 3.4 The masked palm civet (whose technical name is *Paguma larvata*) is a small animal related to the mongoose. Its natural habitat ranges from Asia's Himalayan Mountains to Indonesia. In many parts of Asia, and particularly in China, the masked palm civet is considered a gourmet delicacy. Because this creature has been shown to have antibodies to SARS-like viruses, scientists believe the disease may have been spread to humans when people ate contaminated civets.

human SARS isolates have been found in Guangdong from apparently healthy masked palm civets (Figure 3.4), a cat-like mammal closely related to the mongoose. It is possible that people first got SARS by eating these local animals.

THE SEARCH FOR THE CAUSE OF SARS

Dr. Malik Peiris and his colleagues at the University of Hong Kong were the first to identify a new type of coronavirus from two patients with SARS. They then found evidence of the same virus in 90% of the 50 patients they studied. The new coronavirus, which is responsible for SARS, is called SARS-CoV, short for SARS–human coronavirus.

A number of laboratories across the world undertook the job of determining the identity of the pathogen that was causing SARS. The virus isolation was performed on a specimen from a person from the original case cluster from Toronto, Canada, who had died of the disease. A bronchoalveolar lavage was performed. This is a process in which water is squirted into the respiratory tract and then the fluid is suctioned out and cultured in a growth medium to search for any pathogens that may be living in the respiratory tract. The National Microbiology Laboratory in Canada isolated the virus from a patient in Toronto and succeeded in growing a coronavirus-like agent in African green monkey cells.

This coronavirus was named publicly by the World Health Organization and cooperating laboratories on April 16, 2003, as the "SARS virus." The efforts of laboratories from 10 countries, together with WHO, helped speed up the identification of the SARS virus after the test of causation, including monkey inoculation. To prove causation—that is, to declare definitively that the new coronavirus was the cause of SARS—the virus had to go through all four of Koch's Postulates for proving the causation of disease. As you will recall, the pathogen must be found in all cases of the disease, must be isolated from the host and grown in pure culture, must reproduce the original disease when introduced into a susceptible host, and must be found in the experimental host that was infected. In SARS patients, the novel coronavirus has been found in patients' bodily fluids. The virus has been cultured in an artificial culture. The serum of patients shows antibodies to the virus, and finally, the cultured virus produces disease in monkeys (macaque monkeys). This is the process by which scientists have proven that SARS is caused by the new coronavirus SARS-CoV.

STUDYING THE VIRUS

Research in China and Hong Kong detected several coronaviruses that are closely related genetically to SARS-CoV in two animal species (masked palm civet and raccoon-dog) and antibodies against SARS-CoV in one additional species (Chinese ferret badger). These and other wild animals are traditionally considered delicacies and are sold as food for human consumption in markets throughout southern China. It became obvious to scientists that eating these infected animals was likely what spread the disease to humans. Isolating viruses from these animals indicated that the SARS virus can exist outside of a human host.

Determining the **genome** sequence of the SARS-CoV virus is extremely important to aid in the diagnosis of SARS virus infections in humans and other potential animal hosts. In addition, identifying the SARS genome is also important because it may suggest whether SARS did, in fact, originate in animals, and how transmission of SARS-CoV between species took place. Similar viruses had been identified in some species of animals before the SARS epidemic, but only now had they been isolated in humans, indicating an animal-to-human transmission route. Lastly, knowing the SARS genome helps in the development of antiviral drugs and **vaccines** for the disease because scientists can try to find molecules that block the virus's activity or bind to the virus to make it inactive.

DID SARS START IN ANIMALS?

The genome sequence data of SARS reveal that the new agent does not belong to any of the previously known groups of coronaviruses, including the two known human coronaviruses.

It seems that the new SARS virus supports the hypothesis that it is an animal virus for which the normal host is still unknown and that has recently either developed the ability to infect humans or has been able to cross the species barrier. There is a strong belief based on research in Hong Kong that the virus could have come from the civets sold in Chinese markets to humans, because those civets are born in the wild and then captured and raised in farms. They could therefore have acquired the virus from a wild animal. Despite this information, more research is needed before any firm conclusions can be reached.

4

SARS: Spread and Symptoms

SARS is a communicable disease and a very contagious one that can have fatal consequences (Figure 4.1). Communicable diseases are illnesses that are transmitted directly or indirectly from an infected person or animal through an intermediate animal, host, or vector. (A vector is anything that transmits a disease to another living thing.) The main means by which SARS appears to spread is close person-to-person contact, primarily through the respiratory droplets an infected person produces when he or she coughs or sneezes. The disease can spread when droplets from the cough or sneeze of an infected person are propelled a short distance (generally up to 3 feet [1 meter]) through the air and enter the mouth, nose, or eyes of anyone who happens to be nearby. For infection to occur, however, scientists believe the droplets in the air would have to contain extremely large numbers of the SARS virus. The virus can also spread when a person touches a surface or object that has been contaminated with such infectious droplets and then touches his or her mouth, nose, or eyes.

The airborne spread of SARS—such as from a cough—does not seem to be the major route of transmission, except in situations where people are exposed frequently to massive amounts of pathogens in the air, as occurred in the hospitals where the first SARS patients were treated. **Airborne** (moving by or though the air) **transmission** of the SARS virus is probably a relatively rare event. SARS cases among health-care workers show that most of those infected were exposed to the virus during high-risk activities such as **endotracheal intubation,**

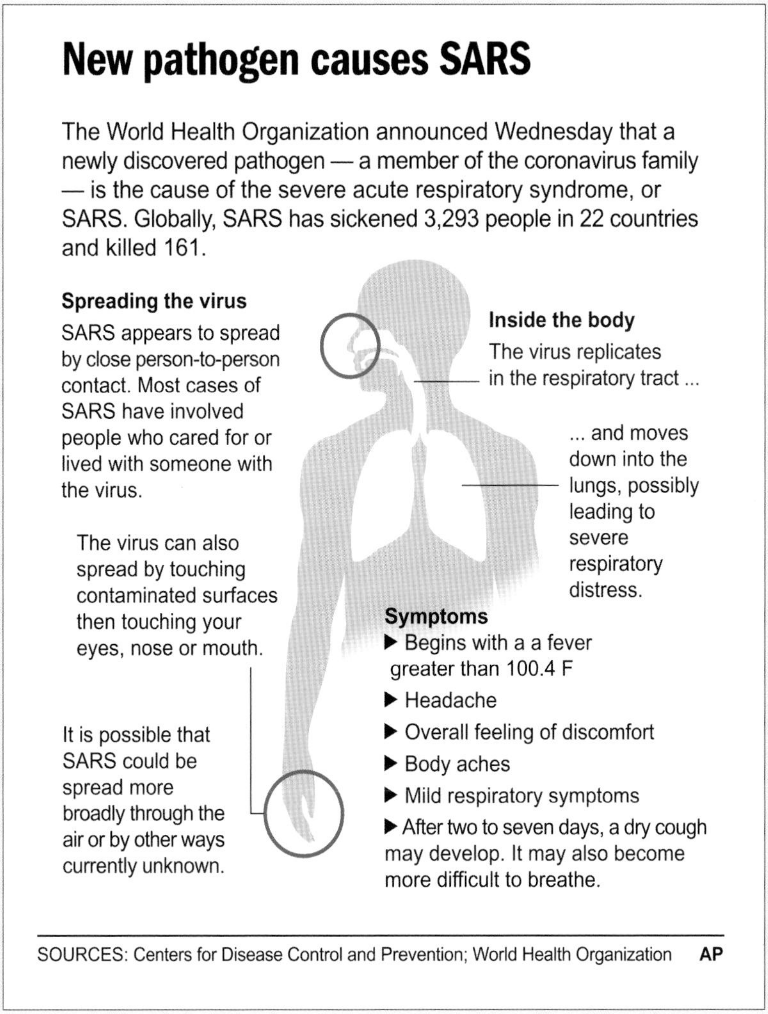

New pathogen causes SARS

The World Health Organization announced Wednesday that a newly discovered pathogen — a member of the coronavirus family — is the cause of the severe acute respiratory syndrome, or SARS. Globally, SARS has sickened 3,293 people in 22 countries and killed 161.

Spreading the virus

SARS appears to spread by close person-to-person contact. Most cases of SARS have involved people who cared for or lived with someone with the virus.

The virus can also spread by touching contaminated surfaces then touching your eyes, nose or mouth.

It is possible that SARS could be spread more broadly through the air or by other ways currently unknown.

Inside the body

The virus replicates in the respiratory tract ...

... and moves down into the lungs, possibly leading to severe respiratory distress.

Symptoms

▶ Begins with a a fever greater than 100.4 F

▶ Headache

▶ Overall feeling of discomfort

▶ Body aches

▶ Mild respiratory symptoms

▶ After two to seven days, a dry cough may develop. It may also become more difficult to breathe.

SOURCES: Centers for Disease Control and Prevention; World Health Organization   **AP**

Figure 4.1 This illustration from the Centers for Disease Control and Prevention was originally published soon after the World Health Organization first announced the discovery of the coronavirus that causes SARS. The diagram provides some valuable details about the symptoms and spread of SARS.

bronchoscopy, and **sputum induction**. This means that it is suspected that they contracted the disease from the instruments used on SARS patients, not directly through the air from patients themselves.

EXPOSURE TO SARS

In the context of SARS, close contact means having cared for or lived with someone infected with SARS or having a high likelihood of direct contact with the respiratory secretions and/or body fluids of a patient known to have SARS. Examples include kissing or embracing, sharing eating or drinking utensils, talking to someone within a space of about 3 feet, physical examination, and any other direct physical contact between people. Close contact does not include activities such as walking past a person or briefly sitting across from someone in a waiting room or office.

The presence of the SARS virus in the stool suggests that **oral-fecal transmission** is also one possibility. An outbreak in an apartment complex in Hong Kong that accounted for more than 300 cases was attributed to fecal spread. As you'll recall from Chapter 1, the SARS-CoV is stable in feces (and urine) at room temperature for at least 1 to 2 days.

Part of what determines whether someone who is exposed to SARS will get sick is the size of the **inoculum**—that is, the number of infectious particles that are transmitted from the infected person to the healthy person. The size of the inocolum is determined by the **viral load** (number of viruses) in the secretion of the **index patient** and the distance the healthy person is from the index patient. When someone first contracts SARS, the viral load is relatively low for the first few days after the onset of symptoms. The viral load increases gradually, peaking on the 10th day after the first symptoms appear. This suggests that SARS patients may be most contagious around the 10th day of the disease. They may be more or less likely to spread the illness the rest of the time, even during the symptomatic phase of the disease. Transmission is more likely to happen in the later phase of the illness.

SYMPTOMS

The first symptoms of SARS are nonspecific—which means that they are very similar to the symptoms of many other diseases. This makes it hard for doctors to make a diagnosis. Symptoms start out with flu-like complaints, including high fever (above 100.4°F, or 38.0°C). This fever is often accompanied by headaches, malaise (a general feeling of being unwell), chills, and diarrhea.

Because these common symptoms make it difficult to distinguish SARS from an ordinary infection of the airways, such as bronchitis, doctors have to do a clinical examination of the patient along with radiological (X-ray) and laboratory tests to tell if the person really does have SARS. Anyone who comes down with flu-like symptoms and has had prior contact with someone known to have SARS, or has traveled to a geographic location where SARS is relatively common, should seek medical attention immediately upon noticing symptoms.

WHO CAN SPREAD SARS?

For easy and efficient transmission of the SARS virus, the "ideal" conditions would be to have a patient who is highly infectious, shedding (passing out of the body through the breath, urine, or feces) large quantities of infectious virus. The patient must also have comorbidities (other illnesses) that mask the symptoms and signs of SARS. Patients with other chronic conditions and weakened immune systems will be most vulnerable. Finally, the patient has to be admitted to a hospital and be put into contact with multiple persons through the process of doing the diagnostic tests, possibly including high-risk procedures such as bronchoscopy, intubation, and use of **nebulizers.**

It is still unclear whether someone who is infected but asymptomatic can infect others. There is no direct evidence that transmission of SARS has ever occurred from an asymptomatic person. Indirect evidence that this may occur in rare cases includes a report that tracing contacts of SARS patients in Hong Kong failed to identify a known symptomatic SARS patient in a small percentage of reported cases. But this could also be a result of an incomplete search for contacts.

Scientists generally believe that only patients who currently show symptoms may spread the SARS virus efficiently. However, transmission appears not to happen in an explosive way. Some 81% of all probable SARS patients in Singapore showed no evidence that they had spread SARS or any other clinically identifiable illness to other people.

This information fits with observations from the early Toronto outbreak, when suspected cases in which people did not seem to have pneumonia were initially sent home to spend their time in isolation. Some patients did not adhere to the isolation requirements and went out and interacted with the community. Despite this fact, apart from an outbreak among a religious group, no additional disease turned up in the community. Also, a report from the Philippines describes a patient who began to show symptoms on April 6, had close contact with 254 family members and friends, traveled extensively through the Philippines, and attended a prayer meeting and a wedding before being hospitalized on April 12. The people with whom the patient had been in contact were placed under home quarantine for 9 days, with twice-daily temperature monitoring by health workers to help authorities determine if any new cases turned up that could be traced back to the first patient. Elevated temperature is the first warning sign. Of all the exposed contacts, only two individuals developed SARS. This figure represents an infection rate of less than 1% for contacts made outside of the hospital setting. Compared with other infectious diseases that may be spread via the respiratory route—for example, influenza—SARS seems to be only moderately transmissible through the air.

SUPERSPREADING

The term *superspreading* has been used to describe situations in which a single individual has directly infected a large number of other people. In the Singapore epidemic, of the first 201 probable SARS cases reported, 103 of the patients had been infected by just 5 source patients.

A common feature of superspreading is **nosocomial** (infection acquired in the hospital) transmission, with hospitals serving as sources for the spread and increase in severity of the disease. The most probable explanation for the phenomenon of superspreading is extensive viral shedding by particular patients. Any infected patient releases virus into the environment around them as he or she breathes. This is referred to as "viral shedding." Some people may release much higher quantities of the virus than others, though, perhaps because they are in an advanced stage of the disease or have other illnesses that allow the virus to multiply even faster than usual.

RECOGNIZING AN ILLNESS AS SARS

Unrecognized cases of SARS have been implicated in outbreaks in Singapore, Taiwan, and Toronto. Despite efforts to implement extensive control measures, these outbreaks happened, and spread to other health-care facilities. Several factors might contribute to the difficulties in recognizing cases of SARS. For one, early SARS symptoms are nonspecific and patients may seem to be suffering from other, more common illnesses. Moreover, patients may have chronic conditions, and their SARS symptoms might be attributed to those underlying diseases. Finally, some patients might not reveal useful information for fear of being stigmatized—that is, feeling ashamed of having the disease. These experiences demonstrate that the spread of SARS among health-care workers can occur despite medical professionals' superior knowledge about how SARS is transmitted.

There has been at least one report of SARS-CoV transmission during quarantine. Family contacts of a SARS patient became infected during hospital quarantine because

HISTORY OF QUARANTINE

The practice of quarantine began during the 14th century as an attempt to protect coastal cities from plague epidemics and other infectious diseases, particularly from the East. Ships arriving in Venice, Italy, and ports along the Adriatic Sea were required to sit at anchor for 40 days before they were allowed to land. The isolation of ships, including passengers and goods, was a mandatory procedure. This practice, called "quarantine," was derived from the Latin word *quaresma*, meaning "40."

When the United States first gained its independence from Great Britain in the late 1700s, little was done to prevent the importation of infectious diseases. Although some attempts were made to impose quarantine requirements, protections against imported diseases were considered a local matter and handled by the individual states. It was because of severe yellow fever epidemics that Congress finally passed the Federal Quarantine Legislation in 1878.

Today, the Division of Global Migration and Quarantine is part of the CDC's National Center for Infectious Diseases and is headquartered in Atlanta, Georgia. Quarantine stations are located in Atlanta, New York, Miami, Chicago, Los Angeles, San Francisco, Seattle, and Honolulu. Quarantine operations involve the cooperation of several agencies, including state and local health agencies, Customs and Border Protection, the U.S. Department of Agriculture (USDA), and the Bureau of Citizenship and Immigration Services.

Figure 4.2 During the SARS outbreak in Asia, people who had the illness, or were believed to have been exposed to it, were isolated from others to avoid spreading the disease. Although these steps were important in stopping the epidemic from becoming a global problem, they often caused fear among the general public. Seen here is an Asian man, peering out from the gates inside which he has been quarantined as part of SARS control measures.

strict isolation was not enforced. Patients diagnosed with SARS may or may not be infected with the SARS virus, but they are certainly at risk of contracting the infection if they are grouped with known infected SARS patients. Therefore, isolation is mandatory (Figure 4.2). How long patients should remain in isolation depends on whether and to what extent they continue to shed the virus from their respiratory tract or feces after obvious clinical symptoms such as coughing have stopped. Currently, at least 14 days of home quarantine are recommended after a suspected SARS patient is discharged from the hospital.

5

Diagnosis and Management of SARS

The clinical diagnosis of SARS remains based on epidemiological background, clinical manifestations, and differentiation of the disease from other infections. The epidemiological portion of the diagnosis looks for possible avenues through which the disease might have spread—for example, if the patient traveled to China or danced with a known SARS patient. Lack of reliable, standardized tests for SARS virus **antibody** detection makes diagnosis difficult, to say the least. Until reliable tests and methods are adequately field tested, diagnosis will continue to be arduous and lengthy for doctors.

Humans have an immune system to protect them from the negative consequences of infections. As mentioned earlier, antibodies are small proteins that the human body develops to counter the presence of foreign organisms such as viruses or bacteria. Natural immunity is acquired when a patient has a disease and recovers from it. For example, if you have had the measles, you are not likely to contract it again because your body has produced antibodies to protect you against the measles virus. These antibodies often provide protection for the rest of your life. Vaccines provide the same protection, but with the benefit of not having to experience the disease. A vaccine injects a weakened or killed pathogen into the body—usually not enough to cause disease symptoms, but enough to start an immune response that will produce antibodies to fight the disease, should it ever confront or challenge the body again.

TESTING FOR SARS

There is no single test that can be used to diagnose SARS with accuracy. Therefore, diagnosis relies on a doctor's clinical examination, supported by case definitions that include a travel history. When a person is infected with SARS, it may take between 2 and 10 days for symptoms to appear. This is typically the virus's **incubation period**—the time between the entry of the disease organism into the body and when symptoms first show up. After the initial symptoms, either the disease subsides, or it progresses to a severe respiratory phase. This second phase is dangerous and can lead to acute respiratory failure and death. The respiratory phase starts within 2 to 4 days of the onset of fever. A dry, nonproductive cough develops and may be accompanied by shortness of breath. This usually takes place during the second week of the illness. Sometimes SARS progresses to a generalized infection of the lung, and the patient requires intubation (the passing of a tube into the lung so that oxygen may be provided to ease breathing difficulty) just to survive. Mechanical ventilation may also be needed. In such cases, a machine sends oxygen under pressure into the lungs and removes the carbon dioxide forcibly from the respiratory system. In severe cases, like that of Dr. Carlo Urbani, even these measures may not be enough to save the person's life.

RISK FACTORS

SARS is very contagious. People with SARS are most likely infectious when they have symptoms of the disease such as fever and cough. It is not known for how long they are infectious before their symptoms begin, or how infectious they may be. There are risk factors that can increase the probability that someone will contract the disease. People at a higher risk, as previously mentioned, include older persons with chronic conditions and health-care workers who have direct contact with SARS patients.

A person may be at greater risk if he or she has cared for, lived with, or been in direct contact with the respiratory secretions and/or body fluids of a person suspected of having SARS. In the case of health workers, they have to take precautionary measures and follow specific SARS care guidelines. The CDC as well as the Canadian Health Authorities developed recommendations to prevent the transmission of respiratory pathogens to health-care workers as they perform procedures that carry the risk of being infected by the ill patient (Figure 5.1). When caring for SARS patients, health-care workers are urged to:

- Use gloves

- Wear an N95 mask (a special surgical mask designed to filter the air before the person wearing the mask inhales, to keep out any pathogens that may be carried through the air)

- Use eye protection

- Wear gowns

- Follow scrupulous hand hygiene (washing with both soap and alcohol).

Also, the above protective materials must be properly discarded and replaced if necessary before the health-care worker visits another patient.

The rapid spread of SARS among health-care workers in Hanoi, Vietnam, and in hospitals in Hong Kong confirmed the potentially highly contagious nature of the SARS virus. Medical personnel, physicians, nurses, and hospital workers were among those commonly infected. Attack rates in excess of 50% have been reported among health workers who treated SARS patients. SARS infection of health-care workers is probably related to increased contact with respiratory secretions, contact with patients during the most contagious phase of

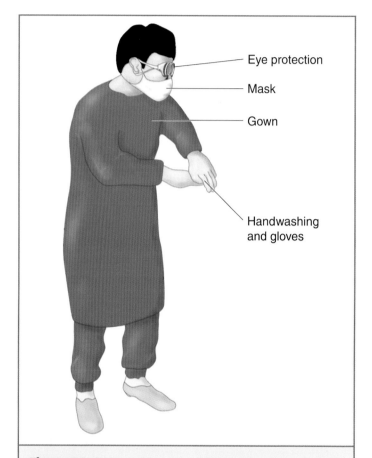

Eye protection

Mask

Gown

Handwashing
and gloves

Figure 5.1 At the height of the SARS outbreak, many people tried to take every possible precaution to avoid contracting the disease. Although certain safety procedures (including wearing safety gear like that shown in this illustration) were recommended for those at high risk of becoming infected, such as hospital workers, ordinary people were often seen wearing surgical masks and gloves while going about their daily business. This misunderstanding of how SARS is spread likely made the widespread panic over the disease even worse.

critical illness, and/or contact with particular patients who have an increased likelihood (for instance, due to other diseases) of spreading SARS.

Diagnostic and therapeutic procedures inside the hospital, such as diagnostic sputum induction, bronchoscopy, endotracheal intubation, and airway suction are potent aerosol-generating procedures and are now recognized as high-risk activities for hospital personnel and visitors.

Obviously, hospital workers must use precautions. But SARS can still occur despite knowledge about epidemiology and transmission of the virus. To reduce the number of unrecognized cases, the Singapore Ministry of Health recommended

DO SURGICAL MASKS STOP SARS?

The dramatic photos of people walking the streets of Asian cities wearing surgical masks suggest that these masks might be a good **prophylactic** and protection against the disease.

Although the CDC does advise people who have SARS to wear these masks, they do not recommend them for people in contact with those patients unless the infected person can't wear one him- or herself. Wearing surgical masks outdoors, where virus-laden particles easily disperse, even through the fabric of the mask, has even less value.

The CDC does advise health-care workers involved with SARS patients to wear a special mask called an N95 respirator. But even these masks offer limited protection from coronaviruses. The "95" in the name of the device means that, if the mask is properly fitted, it can filter particles as small as 0.3 microns 95% of the time. Human coronaviruses measure between 0.1 and 0.2 nitrons, which is one to two times smaller than the cutoff size. Properly fitted, the N95 mask seems to offer better protection than nothing, but is not a guarantee that the wearer will not become infected with SARS.

To efficiently protect yourself against coronaviruses, you would need to wear a full-faced mask with a high-efficiency particle air filter.

a strategy to quickly identify **febrile** (having a high fever) or symptomatic persons with chronic illnesses or any recent health-care facility contact as a suspected case for isolation. Following strict isolation procedures is very important in decreasing the spread of SARS.

There is no indication that SARS can spread widely through a community, since close contact has to occur to assist the spread of the disease. Therefore, when patients with SARS are identified and placed in quarantine, strict isolation should be observed. The report of three family members of a SARS patient who became infected during a hospital quarantine that was not observed properly was a costly lesson in how strictly isolation measures must be carried out when dealing with SARS. Patients diagnosed with SARS may or may not actually be infected with the SARS virus, but even if they are not infected, they are at risk of contracting the disease if they are housed with infected patients.

Health-care facilities should emphasize the importance of infection control measures for respiratory infections, and if there is a good reason for doctors and the health department to suspect a person might have SARS, then the patient should immediately be placed on SARS isolation precautions, and all contacts with the ill patient should be identified, evaluated, and monitored for signs of infection.

Additionally, extreme caution has to be taken in the handling and consumption of exotic animals in parts of the world where such creatures are considered culinary delicacies. As you will recall, SARS-CoV was found in three animal species taken from a market in southern China (masked palm civet, raccoon-dog, and Chinese ferret badger). Antibody studies in people working in markets that sell these animals show that they have a higher antibody **prevalence** in comparison with the general population. As a precautionary measure, persons who might come into contact with these species or their products, including body fluids and excretions, should be aware of the possible health risks, mostly during close contact such as handling and slaughtering, and possibly also food processing and consumption.

Another risk to be avoided is traveling to countries affected by SARS outbreaks. To date, the areas with the greatest number of SARS cases include China, Singapore, Canada (the Toronto area), and Vietnam.

DIAGNOSIS

The diagnosis of SARS-CoV disease and the implementation of control measures should be based on the degree of the patient's risk of exposure. According to CDC guidelines, in the absence of any person-to-person transmission of SARS-CoV worldwide, the overall likelihood that a patient being evaluated for fever or respiratory illness has SARS will be exceedingly low unless there are both typical clinical findings and some additional epidemiological evidence that raises suspicion that the person has been exposed to SARS-CoV. Perhaps, only patients who require hospitalization for unexplained pneumonia and who have an epidemiological history that raises the suspicion of SARS exposure, such as recent travel to a previously known SARS-affected area or close contact with an ill person with such a travel history, should even be considered for a SARS diagnosis. Suspicions should also arise when health workers who have had direct patient contact, a technician in a laboratory that works with live SARS-CoV, or someone with an epidemiological link to a cluster of cases of unexplained pneumonia shows the symptoms typical of SARS. Figure 5.2 illustrates the algorithm (instructions) for evaluation and management of patients who are hospitalized for X-ray–confirmed pneumonia.

CONFIRMING THE DIAGNOSIS

To confirm a SARS diagnosis, several tests have to be performed. A complete blood test is necessary because, during the course of illness, abnormal blood values are common. **Lymphopenia**

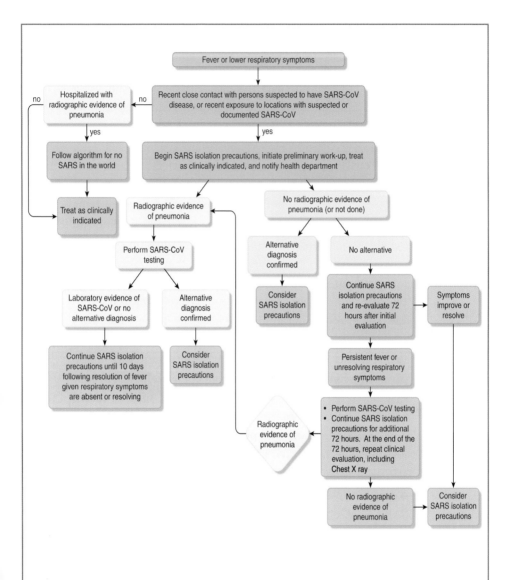

Figure 5.2 The efficient cooperation among global health agencies helped stop the spread of SARS before it could kill hundreds of thousands or even millions, and put into place procedures to follow when dealing with suspected SARS cases. This chart shows the steps medical professionals are supposed to follow when they are trying to determine whether a patient who shows a fever or lower respiratory symptoms (see top of chart) may, in fact, have SARS.

(an abnormal lowering of the blood's white cell count) and **thrombocytopenia** (an abnormally low number of thrombocytes, or platelets) are frequent. Transient **leukopenia** (an abnormal reduction in the number of white blood cells) is also found in patients during their first weeks of illness. In addition, a great number of patients also have low calcium, phosphorus, magnesium, sodium, and potassium levels. Elevated levels of lactate dehydrogenase and aspartate have also been mentioned in studies, and these levels are used to help further confirm a SARS infection. It remains unclear whether these abnormalities reflect the natural course of the SARS infection or whether they occur because of the effects of treatment with agents that influence renal function—that is, the kidney's ability to do its job.

Additional tests to help confirm a diagnosis of possible SARS cases are necessary. For example, chest X rays are used to identify pneumonia. Influenza tests and blood cultures are needed to eliminate the possibility that the illness is being caused by the growth of other microorganisms. All parameters involved in the diagnosis are important. In the case of SARS, both the clinical examination and the radiological and laboratory tests are of the utmost importance, as is a travel history and history of contact with possible SARS cases.

Isolating the SARS virus is another test that must be done to indicate the presence of live SARS-CoV. The virus can be detected by inoculating suitable cell cultures with patients' cultures (such as respiratory secretion, blood, or stool) and growing the virus *in vitro* (outside the body; often referring to the laboratory setting). Once isolated, the virus must be identified as SARS-CoV through further tests (Figure 5.3). If the cell culture results indicate that SARS is present in the sample tested, the patient is diagnosed with SARS. However, negative cell culture results do not necessarily mean that the person does not have SARS, because, as previously stated, the test is not 100% accurate in identifying all cases, especially early ones in which the patient may have a low viral load.

Figure 5.3 Once the virus that is responsible for causing SARS was identified and isolated, it became easier to determine whether a particular person was suffering from SARS or from some other respiratory illness. Before making a definitive diagnosis of SARS, health-care professionals must take samples of blood, sputum, or other body fluids from the patient and subject them to many tests to confirm that the SARS virus is present. Test strips like this one will show a color change to indicate whether the virus is present or not.

SARS CASE DEFINITION

To classify patients with unexplained pneumonia that raise a suspicion of SARS, the World Health Organization has come out with guidelines for a SARS case definition.

As defined by the World Health Organization, there are currently two SARS classification categories: suspected cases and probable cases.

A *suspected case* is classified as a disease

- in a person with a documented fever (temperature greater than 98.6°F/38°C);

- lower respiratory tract symptoms, such as pneumonia;

- close contact with a person believed to have had SARS during the 10 days prior to the onset of symptoms;

- or a history of travel to a geographic area where there has been documented transmission of the illness.

A *probable case* is a suspected case with:

- chest X-ray findings of pneumonia;

- acute respiratory distress syndrome (RDS); or

- an unexplained respiratory illness resulting in death with autopsy findings that seem to show the person had RDS without an identifiable cause.

The CDC has added laboratory criteria for evidence of infection with SARS-CoV to its current surveillance case definition. Using these criteria, a SARS case is considered laboratory-confirmed if one of the following criteria is met:

- detection of antibodies to SARS-associated coronavirus in a serum sample;

- detection of SARS-CoV RNA by **RT-PCR** confirmed by a second PCR (polymerase chain reaction) assay, by using a second sample of the specimen and a different set of PCR primers; or

- isolation of SARS-CoV.

Negative laboratory results for PCR, viral culture, or antibody tests obtained within 28 days of illness do not rule out a coronavirus infection, perhaps even the coronavirus that causes SARS.

TESTING FOR SARS

Once the World Health Organization declared that a new coronavirus was the pathogen responsible for SARS, Chinese researchers started to develop specific tests to diagnose SARS. Even though various tests have been developed by different groups around the world, and one of them is available commercially, the results of these tests should still not be used to rule out a suspected case of SARS, according to current WHO recommendations.

In many viral diseases, virus shedding is greatest during the early symptomatic phase—that is, around and immediately following the initial onset of symptoms. Unfortunately, virus excretion is comparatively low during the early phases of SARS. Instead, shedding peaks in respiratory specimens and in stool at around day 10 after the onset of symptoms. For an early diagnosis, it is therefore necessary to use highly sensitive tests that are able to detect even very low levels of the virus during the first days of illness. The tests currently available do not detect the small amounts of SARS coronavirus initially shed, and therefore, they do not play a role in patient management or case control, since SARS patients may be capable of infecting others during the early phase and must be reliably identified and quickly isolated.

In response to infection with SARS-CoV, different types of antibodies appear and change in level during the course of the infection. Various methods have been developed for the detection of these antibodies, which remain undetectable in the early stages of infection.

PROBLEMS WITH SARS TESTING

All tests for SARS-CoV that are available at this time have

limitations. Extreme caution is therefore necessary when patient management decisions must be based on virological test results. SARS-CoV testing should be considered if no alternative diagnosis is made within 72 hours after the clinical evaluation has begun and the patient is thought to be at high risk for SARS. Health-care providers should immediately report all positive SARS-CoV test results to the local or state health department. Testing to confirm a SARS diagnosis at an appropriate test site should be arranged through the local or state health department.

6

Treatment of SARS

Prevention and control of SARS-CoV transmission in the community are still the most effective ways to stop this often-fatal infectious disease (Figure 6.1). Prevention and control rely on prompt identification and management of both SARS patients and their contacts. This approach has so far proven to be the best treatment, due to the absence of a specific SARS vaccine or a definitive treatment. When a vaccine or effective antiviral agent become available in the future, they will, naturally, become the treatment and prevention options of choice.

MANAGING SARS

Countries that face SARS outbreaks have implemented classic public health measures, including case detection, isolation, infection control, and contact tracing to successfully treat the epidemic. In addition, population screening for the early detection of SARS, with the use of a tool as simple as a thermometer, supported by mass public education and information campaigns, were decisive in avoiding the further spread of the disease.

Isolation

Isolation refers to separating infected people from healthy people and restricting the infected patients' movement to stop the spread of the illness to otherwise healthy people. It is used for patients who are known to have the SARS illness. Isolation allows for the focused delivery of specialized health care to people who are ill, and it protects healthy people from getting sick. People in isolation may be cared for in their homes, in hospitals, or in specially designated health-care facilities.

Figure 6.1 Despite scientific evidence that surgical masks are ineffective at preventing the spread of airborne particles of the SARS virus, during the height of the SARS epidemic, people all over the world—particularly in Asia, where the most infections occurred—regularly wore masks to try to protect themselves whenever they went out in public, as these Asian schoolchildren are doing.

Quarantine

Quarantine, like isolation, is also intended to stop the spread of SARS. Quarantine is used for people who have been exposed to the virus but who may or may not become ill. In quarantine situations, the person who has been exposed, though not yet ill, is separated from other people and kept in a restricted area, because he or she may still become infectious. During the 2003 global SARS outbreak, patients in the United States were quarantined until they were no longer infectious. This practice allowed patients to receive appropriate care, and it helped contain the spread of the illness. Seriously ill patients were cared for in hospitals, while persons with mild illness were cared for at home. Those being cared for at home were asked to avoid contact with other people and to remain at home until 10 days after any fever and respiratory symptoms had fully gone away.

Medications

In addition to controlling the spread of SARS, when confronted with specific SARS cases, doctors have a wide range of medicines they can prescribe. To treat people already infected with the SARS virus, several treatments have been used with a certain degree of success. Nevertheless, the lack of an effective specific treatment for SARS has been frustrating, and the search for a safe and definitive treatment continues to be a major challenge for scientists even now that the SARS epidemic has been contained.

Antibiotics

Among the first and most often prescribed types drugs to treat SARS cases are **antibiotics**. Even though SARS itself is caused by a virus and cannot be killed by antibiotics, antibiotic therapy is routinely prescribed for SARS patients to protect against common respiratory pathogens that may make the original illness worse. In addition to their **antibacterial** effects, some antibiotics are known to have **immunomodulatory** (helping to regulate the immune system) properties.

Antibiotics are relatively new drugs. The first anti-infective agents were the sulfa drugs developed around 1940. They were widely used for various infections, such as earaches.

The penicillins, developed shortly thereafter, were considerably better at treating a broader spectrum of bacterial diseases. Derivatives of those early penicillins are still used

THE DISCOVERY OF ANTIBIOTICS

The success of antibiotics in attacking bacteria can be considered one of modern medicine's greatest achievements. First used frequently during World War II (1939–1945), antibiotics have saved many lives and reduced or even eliminated some complications of long-feared diseases and infections.

During the late 19th century, people began to accept the germ theory of disease, which stated that bacteria and other microorganisms were the cause of disease and illness. Scientists thus began to search for substances that could kill these "germs" and rid the body of the disease. One of the pioneers who showed that harmless bacteria could treat disease was Louis Pasteur. He demonstrated that the bacterial disease anthrax could be thwarted in animals by a simple injection of bacteria found in common soil. Following Pasteur's discovery, a German scientist by the name of E. de Freudenreich extracted a substance from a type of bacteria that was found to act as an antibiotic.

In 1928, the British scientist Alexander Fleming had a breakthrough. One night, he left some Petri dishes on which he had been growing *Staphylococcus* bacteria out in his laboratory. When he returned to the lab, he noticed that there were certain areas of the plate where no bacteria appeared. A cluster of blue-green mold called *Penicillium* was growing on the plate near the area where the bacteria were absent. Through additional research, Fleming was able to show that a chemical substance in the mold was lethal to *Staphylococcus* bacteria. This substance, once extracted from the mold, was named "penicillin" after the mold that led Fleming to his discovery.

today. Antibiotics are the only drugs that actually cure patients of bacterial illnesses. Other drugs just provide relief or control symptoms.

Antiviral Drugs

In addition to antibiotics, **antiviral** agents have also been prescribed from the outset of the SARS epidemic. Their use has continued despite lack of evidence about whether they are actually effective. With the discovery of the SARS-CoV as the pathogen that causes SARS, scientific research institutions worldwide have been vigorously attempting to develop a useful antiviral agent to treat the disease.

For example, the drug ribavirin was widely used as an empirical therapy for SARS because of its broad-spectrum antiviral activity against both DNA and RNA viruses. The use of ribavirin has brought about much criticism because its usefulness has not been proven and because it has considerable side effects. Side effects such as hemolytic anemia (low red blood cell count) and rises in transaminase (a liver enzyme that can potentially signal liver function problems when elevated) are dose-related.

Corticosteroids

Another treatment commonly used for SARS patients is corticosteroids (synthetic, more powerful agents than the naturally occurring cortisone). Corticosteroids have been the mainstay of immunomodulatory therapy for SARS. Their timely use often led to early improvement in terms of making fever subside and improving the patient's ability to take in and use oxygen. However, there is much skepticism and controversy about the use of corticosteroids, centering on their effectiveness, their negative effects (including the suppression of the immune system), and their impact on final patient outcomes. The timing of using corticosteroids for SARS patients should coincide with the onset of a truly excessive immune response;

otherwise, the weakened immune system could actually make the patient's condition worse. The duration and dosage of corticosteroids also has to be closely monitored.

Herbal Remedies

In China, traditional herbal medicine has been frequently used in conjunction with Western medicine to treat SARS. Glycyrrhizin, which is derived from licorice roots, is sometimes believed to be effective against SARS when given in very high concentrations. Again, data from clinical trials about how well glycyrrhizin works are lacking. Therefore, no one can be certain at this point if the herb is really effective and, if it is, how exactly it works.

Interferons and Immunoglobulins

Lastly, doctors may treat SARS with human interferons and human immunoglobulins (a substance found in the blood in tiny quantities that provides immunological protection; the best-known of these is gamma-globulin). Human interferons are a family of cytokines important in the cellular immune response. Anecdotal studies have shown that patients recover faster when interferon is used in combination with immunoglobulins. Human gamma immunoglobulins were used to treat SARS in some hospitals in China and Hong Kong. Many times, these medicines are used in conjunction with corticosteroids. Their effectiveness in treating SARS remains uncertain at this stage.

WORKING TOWARD A VACCINE

A huge break in the treatment and, therefore, in the control of SARS patients has been the recent testing of a SARS vaccine on humans (Figure 6.2). Chinese scientists have begun to test a SARS vaccine on four volunteers at a Beijing hospital. This vaccine was jointly developed by the Chinese Ministry of Sciences and Technology and a local company. The Chinese

Racing to find a SARS vaccine

A vaccine that is created in 15 or 20 years is considered speedy but scientists are hoping to create a vaccine for the SARS virus in just three.

Vaccine development

Research	Pre-clinical evaluations	Clinical trials	Approval
Studies focus on the biological mechanisms of the organism that cause damage to the body.	Vaccine preparations are tested in cell cultures and lab animals. Computer models are sometimes used to visualize the vaccine and its interaction in the body.	Hundreds of human volunteers are given the vaccine. They are frequently tested and evaluated over long periods of time to assess the safety and progress of the vaccine.	The Food and Drug Administration approves a vaccine after it is proven to be safe, effective disease and remains stable and potent during its shelf life.

Traditional vaccines

Type	Description	Used to fight
Inactivated	Dead disease-causing bacteria or virus that stimulates a weak immune system response; must be given more than once.	Influenza, cholera, plague and hepatitis A
Attenuated	Live, weakened version of a virus that is easy for the body to defend against. Usually given only once.	Yellow fever, measles, rubella, mumps

Second-generation vaccines

Type	Description	Used to fight
Conjugate	Parts of a second virus, easily recognized and defeated by the immune system, are linked to the outside of disease-causing bacteria or virus.	Haemophilus influenzae type b (Hib), a type of bacterial meningitis
Subunit	Antigenic fragments of the virus used to evoke an immune system response.	Pneumonia and Hepatitis B*
Recombinant vector	Harmless genetic material from a disease-causing organism is carried inside a weakened second virus.	Currently being tested for use against AIDS and hepatitis B* virus

*A combined recombinant subunit vaccine used

SOURCES: Centers for Disease Control and Prevention; U.S. Department of Health and Human Services   AP

Figure 6.2 Ever since the virus that causes SARS was identified shortly after the initial outbreak in 2003, scientists have been racing to find an effective vaccine that will prevent people from ever getting SARS in the first place. This chart shows the steps that commonly occur in the development of a new vaccine.

vaccine is made from a dead sample of the virus that scientists say causes SARS. According to reports from China, tests of the vaccine on animals have shown it to be effective. A SARS vaccine has also been successfully tested on animals in the United States. However, health authorities, including WHO, say that a safe and effective vaccine for humans in commercial quantities is at least a year away. Teams around the world are racing to develop an effective vaccine for SARS, in case another serious outbreak of the disease resurfaces.

In spite of the great efforts by doctors, scientists, and health authorities, a good and reliable SARS treatment is still

THE FIRST SARS VACCINE TESTED

China became the first country in the world to approve clinical testing of the SARS vaccine on people in May 2004. This news brought great expectations for putting a stop to this highly contagious disease.

Three phases of clinical testing are required before a vaccine can be mass-produced. The first phase is to determine if the vaccine is safe for humans. For this phase, the Chinese vaccine was tested on four healthy volunteers. The vaccine tested on the four volunteers is a SARS virus–free placebo, which means that the SARS virus has been destroyed but that the virus-free vaccine can still help people build up immunity against the disease. The second phase of clinical testing aims to determine whether the vaccine can help people produce the antibodies they need to protect them from SARS. For the third phase, the performance of the vaccine during an outbreak is tested by comparing large groups of people who have the SARS virus and a large group of people without the SARS virus. It is difficult to predict how long it will take the SARS vaccine to go through these phases and ultimately be approved for use in large populations.

elusive. So far, the best way to avoid another epidemic remains prevention and control of SARS-CoV transmission within communities. Implementation of community containment

THE HISTORY OF VACCINES

Have you recently had your tetanus shot? What about the chicken pox vaccine? And although you probably do not remember, you received the measles, mumps, and rubella vaccines when you were a baby. These vaccines prevent you from getting a debilitating or potentially lethal disease. In fact, the smallpox vaccine is no longer given because, through its use, the disease has been completely eradicated. Today, vaccines exist for many diseases, and scientists are currently researching methods to defend against even more scourges.

The form of vaccine that we are familiar with is a relatively modern development, but the theory behind vaccines is much older. In the 15th century, the Chinese would deliberately infect themselves with material from smallpox blisters. By scraping some pus from a smallpox blister (pustule) and rubbing it on a scratch or small cut in their own skin, an uninfected person could induce a mild form of the disease. After the person had recovered, he or she was immune to smallpox. This technique was called *variolation*.

The concept of variolation eventually spread to England and caught the attention of a country doctor named Edward Jenner. Jenner noticed that dairymaids, who often contracted cowpox (a disease similar to, but not as deadly as, smallpox) did not contract smallpox. Jenner took the fluid from a cow-pox pustule and placed it under the skin of a young boy. The young boy fell ill with cowpox, but quickly recovered. Shortly thereafter, Jenner infected the same boy with material from a smallpox pustule. The boy developed a blister at the site of infection but did not get sick. Jenner named his discovery *vaccination*, taking the name from the Latin word *vaca*, which means "cow." Vaccines have since been created to protect people from many diseases.

measures rely on public trust. Community officials can generate public trust by communicating clear messages about the rationale for and the role and duration of community containment measures, and the ways in which affected persons will be supported.

7

Prevention and Public Health Measures

To contain the spread of a contagious illness, such as SARS, public health authorities rely on many strategies. Two of these strategies have already been explained in Chapter 6: isolation and quarantine. Both strategies are partial treatment objectives. Both are common practices in public health, and both aim to control exposure to infected or potentially infected persons. Finally, both may be undertaken voluntarily or imposed by public health authorities. Isolation has been employed in the past to help control tuberculosis.

PUBLIC CONTROL OF SARS

Specific measures of prevention include national measures to contain SARS (Figure 7.1). The main focus of SARS surveillance activities in countries that have had no or very few SARS cases is on the early identification and isolation of patients who are suspected of having SARS. In contrast, countries that are affected by severe SARS outbreaks must immediately take a variety of sometimes unpopular measures to contain the epidemic. Generally, this is done by isolating patients and enforcing quarantine for suspected exposed patients. Other more drastic community measures guided toward containing the epidemic may also be established to prevent transmission from SARS patients, which is a critical component of controlling SARS.

Confirmed SARS patients should be admitted to a health-care facility for isolation only if they have been clinically diagnosed or if isolation at home or in a community facility cannot be achieved safely and effectively.

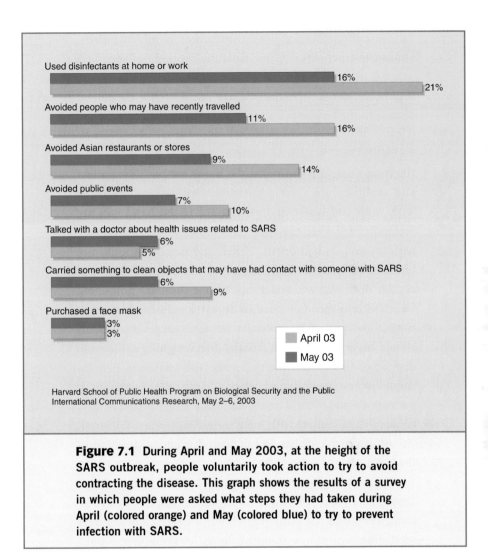

Used disinfectants at home or work
16%
21%

Avoided people who may have recently travelled
11%
16%

Avoided Asian restaurants or stores
9%
14%

Avoided public events
7%
10%

Talked with a doctor about health issues related to SARS
6%
5%

Carried something to clean objects that may have had contact with someone with SARS
6%
9%

Purchased a face mask
3%
3%

April 03
May 03

Harvard School of Public Health Program on Biological Security and the Public International Communications Research, May 2–6, 2003

Figure 7.1 During April and May 2003, at the height of the SARS outbreak, people voluntarily took action to try to avoid contracting the disease. This graph shows the results of a survey in which people were asked what steps they had taken during April (colored orange) and May (colored blue) to try to prevent infection with SARS.

Home isolation is less disruptive to the patient's routine than isolation in a hospital or other community setting. Any patient's home that might be used as an isolation setting should be evaluated by the patient's physician or a local health department official to make sure it is suitable. The best homes for use as isolation centers would have a remotely located bedroom with its own attached bathroom, so that the patient can be completely removed from other family members. During the period of home isolation, household members who are not providing care to the patient should be relocated if possible, so that only the primary caregiver and the patient remain in the residence and vulnerable to the infection.

PREVENTING SARS AT HOME

Infection control measures in the home for both the patient and caregiver are very important to follow. Handwashing with soap and water and an alcohol-based hand rub are recommended after touching body fluids and contaminated surfaces such as bed linens. Towels and bedding should not be shared. These can be cleaned in a washing machine with regular detergent and water, but adding ordinary household bleach is also recommended as an extra measure of protection. Gloves and other protective attire are suggested. Patients should cover the nose and mouth when coughing and should dispose of tissues in a plastic-lined waste container. Patients should wear a surgical mask when other people are present. If patients cannot wear a mask for some reason, people who come in close contact with them should wear a mask instead. Use of disposable dishes and utensils during the duration of the isolation is also recommended.

For people who have been exposed to SARS patients, there should be a vigilant watch for fever and/or respiratory symptoms. People in the same household or other close contacts who show symptoms should follow the same precautions recommended for SARS patients.

PREVENTION METHODS FOR
THE HEALTH-CARE COMMUNITY

The CDC has also prepared guidelines for isolation and precaution for hospitals and health-care facilities in the event that a SARS patient has to be admitted to a hospital. The goals for those health-care facilities are to:

- rapidly identify and isolate all potential SARS patients;

- implement infection control practices;

- trace all contacts to interrupt the spread of SARS-CoV;

- ensure rapid communication within individual health-care facilities;

- and keep communication strong between different health-care facilities and health departments.

BREAKING THE CHAIN OF TRANSMISSION

The goal for infection control in health-care settings, homes, and communities is to recognize patients who are at risk of SARS-CoV disease as early as possible and to prevent the spread of SARS by implementing infection control precautions. In almost all documented cases, transmission of SARS appears to occur through close contact with infected persons. The most effective way to control SARS is to break the chain of transmission from infected to healthy persons. This requires limiting the public interactions of possible or known SARS patients, even if this is unpopular.

THE CENTERS FOR DISEASE CONTROL AND PREVENTION (CDC)

The mission of the Centers for Disease Control and Prevention (CDC) is to protect the health and safety of people both at home and abroad by providing information and collecting data on health, wellness, and disease.

The CDC, which has its main headquarters in Atlanta, Georgia, was organized in 1946 as a branch of the Public Health Service to provide practical help regarding communicable diseases. In the mid-1950s, when polio appeared in children who had received the recently approved Salk vaccine, the

CDC investigated the problem and the national inoculation program was stopped. The cases of polio were traced to contaminated vaccine obtained from a laboratory in California; the problem was corrected, and the inoculation program was resumed. A couple of years later, the CDC again used surveillance to trace the course of a massive influenza epidemic. From the data it gathered in 1957 and subsequent years, the CDC developed national guidelines for influenza vaccine.

As an agency of the Department of Health and Human Services, the CDC's mission is to promote health and quality of life by preventing and controlling disease, injury, and disability. To accomplish its goals, the CDC works with partners in the nation and all over the world to monitor health, detect and investigate health problems, conduct research to enhance disease prevention, develop and advocate sound public health policies, implement prevention strategies, promote healthy behaviors, foster safe and healthful environments, and provide leadership and training.

The Centers for Disease Control and Prevention alone cannot protect the health of the American people. However, by engaging with others—from state and local health departments to private corporations, from media outlets to the general public—the CDC can achieve its vision of a better, safer, and healthier world.

Preventing transmission of SARS through the use of a variety of community containment strategies to maximize success are very important in any public health initiative. Decisions to institute broader community measures takes into consideration the epidemiological characteristics of the SARS outbreak, the health-care resources available, and the level of community cooperation (Figure 7.2).

Figure 7.2 Some of the public health measures implemented to try to stop the spread of SARS were not very popular among local communities. Quarantine and isolation, for example, caused panic in some places, and led to a degree of discrimination against people who came down with SARS. Even less popular were programs in Asia that sprayed germ-killing chemicals in the air, in the hope of killing airborne SARS viruses (as the man in the blue smock is doing in this photograph).

THE NEED FOR NEWS ABOUT SARS

Implementation of all community containment measures relies on public trust. Community officials can help gain public trust by making clear why and how long community containment measures such as quarantines will be in effect.

ASSOCIATED PRESS POLL

Many worry about SARS epidemic

Nearly half of recently polled Americans say they are worried about the possibility of a U.S. SARS epidemic. Yet fewer than 30 percent say they are worried about becoming infected, according to an AP poll.

How worried are you that you or someone in your family will be exposed to SARS?

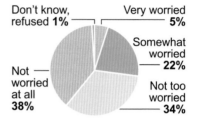

Don't know, refused **1%**
Very worried **5%**
Somewhat worried **22%**
Not worried at all **38%**
Not too worried **34%**

How would you describe the likelihood that a SARS epidemic will spread in this country in the coming months the way it has in some parts of Asia?

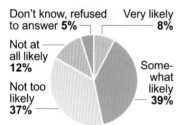

Don't know, refused to answer **5%**
Very likely **8%**
Not at all likely **12%**
Somewhat likely **39%**
Not too likely **37%**

If you or a family member were to get flu-like symptoms such as fever and a bad cough or have trouble breathing, what effect have reports about SARS had on the chances that you would seek medical help?

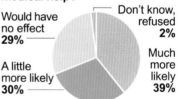

Would have no effect **29%**
Don't know, refused **2%**
A little more likely **30%**
Much more likely **39%**

NOTE: The poll of 1,014 was taken April 25-30 and has an error margin of plus or minus 3 percentage points.

SOURCE: ICR of Media, Pa.   **AP**

Figure 7.3 Although the WHO, CDC, and other public health agencies did a wonderful job of containing the spread of SARS and informing the public about the disease, at times, the way SARS was covered in the media led to exaggerated fears, even in places (like the United States) that had few or no cases of the disease. These graphs show the results of an Associated Press poll from April 2003, in which a large proportion of Americans expressed fear that SARS could become epidemic in the United States.

Nevertheless, there is a balance to be strived for: getting people to show enough concern to follow the necessary guidelines and to report possible suspicious events, but not enough to cause a widespread public panic or a sense of overwhelming hopelessness (Figure 7.3).

8

Impact and Significance of SARS

The impact of SARS on individuals and communities is monumental; from emotional fear, worry, anxiety, shame, guilt over infecting others, concerns about being a burden, blame, and even helplessness, to mass hysteria, social isolation, and discrimination against infected persons and their families. SARS is a new disease that alienates, causes isolation, introduces fear, reinforces discrimination and prejudices, removes one's sense of security, disrupts community mental health, and ultimately has threatened political and economic stability in Asian cities such as Singapore, Beijing, Taipei, and Hong Kong. Within just a week, it made Toronto—formerly a trendy tourist spot—a destination to avoid.

ECONOMIC EFFECTS OF SARS

The considerable economic impact of SARS illustrates the importance that a severe new disease can have on our closely interdependent and highly mobile global community. Published economic costs of the SARS outbreak of 2003, largely based on losses from canceled travel plans and decreased investment in Asia, range from $30 billion to $140 billion. In most of the severely affected areas, service industries and airlines suffered the greatest losses (Figure 8.1). Internationally, a number of trade events excluded participants from Hong Kong and other affected areas.

EFFECTS ON TRAVEL AND TOURISM

As a consequence of the outbreak, many Asian manufacturers lost important opportunities to promote their products in major trade

Airlines strain under impact of war, SARS

The nation's major airlines reported slight improvement last week in slumping traffic figures, as industry officials credited encouraging news out of Iraq. But Pacific region routes suffered an unprecedented decline due to the spread of severe acute respiratory syndrome.

Weekly air traffic growth rates, by destination
Change from same period of previous year

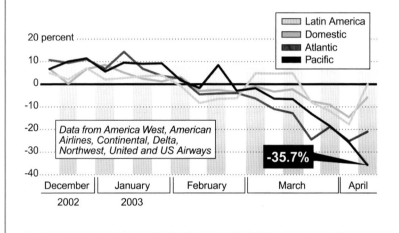

SOURCE: Air Transport Association   **AP**

Figure 8.1 Travel and tourism were hard hit by the SARS epidemic, as people canceled plans to visit places that were known to have cases of the disease. This graph shows the dramatic impact the travel restrictions caused by SARS had on the airline industry from December 2002 through April 2003.

shows around the world. Cutbacks on flights and ship arrivals have had a significant impact on the supply chain of Asian products. SARS has also been responsible for a major dent in Asian tourism.

During the 2003 SARS epidemic, travel restrictions were imposed to prevent the spread of SARS along the routes of international air travel. Travel-related recommendations, even postponing trips, were an important component of the global containment strategy. The objective for governments and local authorities was to collaborate in bringing the outbreak under control. Recommendations concerning travel were ended when epidemiological criteria indicating that there was no longer a high risk to travelers were met. Although there are no SARS-related travel restrictions in place today,

TRAVEL RESTRICTIONS AS A MEASURE TO CONTROL SARS

In coordinating the international response to SARS, the World Health Organization's overriding objective was to prevent SARS from becoming established as a pandemic (worldwide epidemic) disease. Sealing off opportunities for further international spread was a key strategy. As SARS spread along the routes of international air travel, travel-related recommendations were an important component of the global containment strategy.

Although there are no longer any SARS-related travel restrictions in place, it is always best to take precautions before you travel to China or Southeast Asia. For example, to help to protect yourself from infection, wash your hands thoroughly and often. Scrub well with soap or use an alcohol-based hand rub. In China, try not to visit food markets and avoid wildlife, especially civet cats, which are often sold in these markets. Civets have been found to carry viruses similar to the SARS virus. Finally, learn as much as you can about the SARS status of the countries you'll be visiting. You can find information about SARS on the Centers for Disease Control and Prevention and World Health Organization's Websites.

it is always wise to heed safety recommendations when you travel to make sure you enjoy a safe trip.

The World Travel and Tourism Council prepared estimates of the impact of SARS in the Asian region. It is estimated that overall Asian employment faced a decline of between 12 and 41%. Negative impacts on Gross National Product (GNP) and other economic indicators in Asian countries do not capture the full social impact from job losses and company failures in the region. Losses in the tourism industry have repercussions on jobs and growth in other economic sectors. The negative economic impact will continue to be felt for some time, as the number of trips made by foreigners to affected areas in Asia may remain low for years.

Another example of the interconnectedness and inter-dependent nature of our world are the fears expressed in the business press of how supplies of parts for cars, cameras, video gear, and other product components from China could cause production shortfalls in key industries because thousands of workers were at home, ill, or had their factories shut down in Southeast Asia. Officials in those areas are aware that the media need to be kept informed of the measures being taken to enhance travelers' security to gain the confidence of the world community.

THE MEDIA AND PUBLIC PANIC

The media's focus on the virus informed the world and inspired immense international cooperation on research and implementation of control measures such as quarantine and isolation. On the other hand, the media's coverage exaggerated public fear, increasing the growing stigma attached to the illness (Figure 8.2). As a consequence, Chinese neighborhoods were deserted, recovering SARS patients were turned down for jobs, and universities, even in the United States, made it difficult for Asian students to invite their families from back home to attend commencement ceremonies.

Figure 8.2 This photograph of a newly married Asian couple kissing through surgical masks during the height of the SARS outbreak is a poignant example of how the disease caused widespread fear and even what might be considered irrational behavior in those touched by the epidemic.

Media coverage is only one of many elements of the international response. The World Health Organization (WHO) and the Centers for Disease Control and Prevention (CDC) were also responsible for containing the virus. The WHO's activist stance incited a rapid response from countries like Vietnam, which quickly helped curtail the virus's spread. Similarly, the CDC worked closely with airlines, immigration agencies, and airport authorities in the United States and around the world to establish an excellent surveillance system for the disease. This system was the key element in preventing any major SARS outbreaks in the United States. The surveillance cooperation would have spotted any local clusters of infection before they could spread to affect large numbers of people.

SARS has caused considerable social disruption and public anxiety, even in areas well beyond the outbreak sites. Avoidance of travel to certain areas was disproportionate to the risk, as was the widespread wearing of surgical masks. The psychological impact of SARS on health-care workers, affected individuals, their families, and the broader community has not yet been fully evaluated. However, public awareness about SARS had benefited society and all of us in terms of persuading the general public to check frequently for fever and report symptoms promptly. These actions generally reduced the time between onset of symptoms and isolation of patients, thus limiting opportunities for further exposures and transmission.

HOW SARS WAS STOPPED

The significance of SARS as a public health threat is enormous. All new infectious diseases are poorly understood, at least in the beginning of epidemics, and are often associated with high mortality rates. SARS passed readily from person to person, requiring no vector; had no particular geographical affinity; mimicked the symptoms of many other, more mild diseases; took its heaviest toll on hospital workers; and spread internationally with alarming ease. The fact that SARS was contained just a few months after the first global alert, despite the absence of a vaccine, effective treatment, or a reliable diagnostic test, is a great success story for public health. It is also evidence of the willingness of the international community to form a united front against a shared threat.

SARS stimulated an emergency response and a level of media attention on a scale that may have changed public and political perceptions of the risks associated with emerging and epidemic-prone diseases. Reports in scientific publications and the media and from government agencies in several countries agree that SARS raised the profile of public health by demonstrating the severe adverse effects that a health problem can have on economic and social stability, as well as political situations.

WHO is continuing to build on the international networks of real-time collaboration that is improving our understanding of SARS and that helped identify its causative agent early in the outbreak. WHO has also posted guidelines for alert, verification, and public health management of SARS during the post-outbreak period on its Website.

In local areas, health providers and state or local health departments follow guidelines developed by international agencies, cooperate fully, and share information for the well-being of the individual patient as well as the whole community.

GLOBAL AND INDIVIDUAL EFFORTS TO STOP SARS

The reaction to SARS has been a good example of what is possible when health authorities and health-care workers participate cooperatively toward a common goal of education, prevention, and rapid control and treatment of an infectious disease.

A great deal of effort is now being expended on the development of a specific diagnostic test that will be able to tell SARS apart from other respiratory infections. As you might imagine, making a definitive diagnosis sooner would lead to earlier control activities, which should reduce the number of cases in any community. As physicians acquire more experience with SARS and become more familiar with its symptoms, better diagnostic accuracy may be expected.

So far, there is a lot of work being done toward the development of a SARS virus vaccine. Vaccination against viral diseases is an integral part of worldwide communicable disease control. Vaccines against SARS will not only reduce the incidence of the disease, but will also decrease the social and economic burden of the disease on communities and individuals. Illness takes a devastating toll on the patients themselves as well as their communities. Families receive less income when a wage earner cannot work, and when caregivers must also stay home, additional wages are lost. Taken all together, these losses harm tax revenues, industrial production, and the wealth of communities around the world.

In cases where a person contracts a communicable disease such as SARS and has not been immunized, the use of drugs to control the severity of the disease as well as its symptoms becomes extremely important. Effective drugs will likely play a big role in the control and treatment in SARS in coming decades.

The future will surely bring effective and specific vaccines for SARS as well as medications that will decrease symptoms, speed recovery, and perhaps even cure the disease once it starts an infection. When this happens, past experience tells us to be watchful, because people tend to let their guard down when drugs or vaccines become available. We often forget about the dangers of infectious disease and become careless. If this ever happens in regard to SARS, it will be necessary for us to renew our commitment to early identification and treatment.

Appendix I

A Timeline of the SARS Outbreak

November 16, 2002 The first case of atypical pneumonia is reported in the Guangdong province, located in southern China.

February 26, 2003 The first cases of unusual pneumonia are reported in Hanoi, Vietnam.

February 28, 2003 Dr. Carlo Urbani of the World Health Organization (WHO) examines a Chinese-American business-man at a French hospital in Hanoi, Vietnam.

March 10, 2003 Urbani reports an unusual outbreak of the illness, which he names "sudden acute respiratory syndrome," or "SARS," to the main office of the WHO. He states that 22 health-care workers at the hospital have been infected.

March 11, 2003 Health-care workers in Hong Kong fall ill in a similar outbreak of mysterious respiratory disease; Carlo Urbani falls ill.

March 12, 2003 The WHO puts out a global alert, warning the public about the new infectious disease that has been found in both Vietnam and Hong Kong.

March 15, 2003 The WHO issues a global health alert about the disease, and issues a case definition of SARS. Cases in Singapore and Canada are also identified. The alert includes a rare travel advisory for international travelers, medical professionals, and health authorities.

March 17, 2003 An international network of 11 leading research laboratories begin work to determine the cause of SARS.

March 24, 2003 CDC officials offer the first evidence that a new strain of a coronavirus might be the cause of SARS.

March 29, 2003 Carlo Urbani, who identified the first case of SARS, dies from the disease.

April 2, 2003	The WHO issues a travel warning, advising that any nonessential travel to Hong Kong and the Guangdong area of China be postponed.
April 3, 2003	A WHO-sponsored team of infectious disease experts goes to Guangdong to learn more about the outbreak.
April 4, 2003	U.S. President George W. Bush adds SARS to the list of diseases that require suspected patients to be quarantined. This gives the CDC the power to isolate people who might have been exposed to the disease.
April 9, 2003	The WHO investigative team in Guangdong gives its first report. The team says it has found evidence of "superspreaders" who can infect as many of 100 people each.
April 12, 2003	Canadian health researchers announce that they have completed the first successful sequencing of the genome of the coronavirus believed to cause SARS.
April 14, 2003	CDC officials announce that they have sequenced a nearly identical strain of the SARS-related coronavirus.
April 16, 2003	A new form of a coronavirus never before seen in humans is confirmed as the cause of SARS, after being put to the test using Koch's postulates.
April 22, 2003	The CDC issues a health alert for travelers to Toronto, which is the center of the Canadian SARS outbreak.
April 23, 2003	The WHO adds Toronto, Beijing, and the Shanxi province of China to the list of places international travelers should avoid to reduce the risk of contracting SARS. WHO officials say the travel advisory will remain in effect for at least the next three weeks.
April 28, 2003	The WHO removes Vietnam from list of SARS-affected areas, after Vietnam successfully contains its SARS outbreak. The WHO also lifts the travel advisory to Hanoi, Vietnam.

Appendix I

April 29, 2003   The WHO lifts its warning against nonessential travel to Toronto, Canada, after the area has reported no new cases for 20 days.

May 6, 2003   The CDC lifts its travel advisory for Singapore because no new cases of SARS had been reported there for 20 days.

May 15, 2003   The CDC removes its travel alert for Hanoi, Vietnam, after 30 days have passed since the last report of SARS there.

May 17, 2003   The WHO extends its travel warning to include Hebei province, China. A similar warning to cancel or postpone all nonessential travel is in effect for Hong Kong, Taipei, Taiwan, and several other areas of mainland China, including Beijing, Guangdong, Inner Mongolia, Shanxi, and Tianjin.

May 20, 2003   The CDC lifts its travel warning for Toronto, Canada.

May 23, 2003   The WHO lifts its advisory against nonessential travel to Hong Kong and the Guangdong province of China.

May 26, 2003   The WHO lists Toronto, Canada, as an area where SARS has recently been transmitted locally after Canadian health officials report new clusters of 26 suspect and 8 probable SARS cases.

May 31, 2003   The WHO takes Singapore off its list of areas where SARS has been transmitted locally.

June 13, 2003   The WHO lifts its travel restriction on nonessential travel to several provinces in China, including Hebei, Inner Mongolia, Shanxi, and Tianjin.

June 17, 2003   The WHO lifts its travel warning against nonessential travel to Taiwan. The CDC makes its travel warning for mainland China a less-severe alert, although a travel warning from both the CDC and the WHO remains in effect for Beijing.

June 23, 2003	The WHO removes Hong Kong from its list of areas with recent local SARS transmission.
June 24, 2003	The WHO removes its last remaining SARS travel warning for Beijing, China.
June 25, 2003	The CDC downgrades its SARS travel advice for Beijing, China, and Taiwan from "advisory" to "alert" status, which simply informs travelers of a SARS health concern and advises them to take precautions.
July 2, 2003	The WHO removes Toronto, Canada, from its list of areas with recent local SARS transmission.
July 8, 2003	The CDC lifts its SARS travel alert for Toronto, Canada.
July 9, 2003	The CDC lifts its SARS travel alert for Hong Kong retroactively to July 1 because the last SARS case there was reported on May 31.

CDC Fact Sheet
Basic Information About SARS

Available online at *http://www.cdc.gov/ncidod/sars/factsheet.htm.*

SARS

Severe acute respiratory syndrome (SARS) is a viral respiratory illness caused by a coronavirus, called SARS-associated coronavirus (SARS-CoV). SARS was first reported in Asia in February 2003. Over the next few months, the illness spread to more than two dozen countries in North America, South America, Europe, and Asia before the SARS global outbreak of 2003 was contained. This fact sheet gives basic information about the illness and what CDC has done to control SARS in the United States. To find out more about SARS, go to CDC's SARS website and WHO's SARS website.

THE SARS OUTBREAK OF 2003

According to the World Health Organization (WHO), a total of 8,098 people worldwide became sick with SARS during the 2003 outbreak. Of these, 774 died. In the United States, only eight people had laboratory evidence of SARS-CoV infection. All of these people had traveled to other parts of the world with SARS. SARS did not spread more widely in the community in the United States. . . .

SYMPTOMS OF SARS

In general, SARS begins with a high fever (temperature greater than 100.4°F [>38.0°C]). Other symptoms may include headache, an overall feeling of discomfort, and body aches. Some people also have mild respiratory symptoms at the outset. About 10 percent to 20 percent of patients have diarrhea. After 2 to 7 days, SARS patients may develop a dry cough. Most patients develop pneumonia.

HOW SARS SPREADS

The main way that SARS seems to spread is by close person-to-person contact. The virus that causes SARS is thought to be transmitted most readily by respiratory droplets (droplet spread) produced when an infected person coughs or sneezes. Droplet spread can happen when droplets from the cough or sneeze of an infected person are propelled a short distance (generally up to 3 feet) through the air and deposited on the mucous membranes of the mouth, nose, or eyes of persons who are nearby. The virus also can spread when a person touches a surface or object contaminated with infectious droplets and then touches his or her mouth, nose, or eye(s). In addition, it is possible that the SARS virus might spread more broadly through the air (airborne spread) or by other ways that are not now known.

WHAT DOES "CLOSE CONTACT" MEAN?

In the context of SARS, close contact means having cared for or lived with someone with SARS or having direct contact with respiratory secretions or body fluids of a patient with SARS. Examples of close contact include kissing or hugging, sharing eating or drinking utensils, talking to someone within 3 feet, and touching someone directly. Close contact does not include activities like walking by a person or briefly sitting across a waiting room or office.

CDC RESPONSE TO SARS DURING THE 2003 OUTBREAK

CDC worked closely with WHO and other partners in a global effort to address the SARS outbreak of 2003. For its part, CDC took the following actions:

- Activated its Emergency Operations Center to provide round-the-clock coordination and response.

- Committed more than 800 medical experts and support staff to work on the SARS response.

- Deployed medical officers, epidemiologists, and other specialists to assist with on-site investigations around the world.

- Provided assistance to state and local health departments in investigating possible cases of SARS in the United States.

- Conducted extensive laboratory testing of clinical specimens from SARS patients to identify the cause of the disease.

- Initiated a system for distributing health alert notices to travelers who may have been exposed to cases of SARS.

WHAT CDC IS DOING NOW

CDC continues to work with other federal agencies, state and local health departments, and healthcare organizations to plan for rapid recognition and response if person-to-person transmission of SARS-CoV recurs. CDC has developed recommendations and guidelines to help public health and healthcare officials plan for and respond quickly to the reappearance of SARS in a healthcare facility or community.

Preliminary Clinical Description of Severe Acute Respiratory Syndrome
World Health Organization

Severe Acute Respiratory Syndrome (SARS) is a disease of unknown etiology that has been described in patients in Asia, North America, and Europe. The information in this report provides a summary of the clinical characteristics of SARS patients treated in Hong Kong Special Administrative Region (China), Taiwan (China), Thailand, Singapore, the United Kingdom, Slovenia, Canada and the United States since mid-February 2003. This information is preliminary and subject to limitations because of the broad and non-specific case definition.

Most patients identified as of March 21, 2003 have been previously healthy adults aged 25–70 years. A few suspected cases of SARS have been reported among children (≤15 years).

The incubation period of SARS is usually 2–7 days but may be as long as 10 days. The illness generally begins with a prodrome of fever (>38°C), which is often high, sometimes associated with chills and rigors and sometimes accompanied by other symptoms including headache, malaise, and myalgias. At the onset of illness, some cases have mild respiratory symptoms. Typically, rash and neurologic or gastrointestinal findings are absent, although a few patients have reported diarrhea during the febrile prodrome.

After 3–7 days, a lower respiratory phase begins with the onset of a dry, non-productive cough or dyspnea that may be accompanied by or progress to hypoxemia. In 10%–20% of cases, the respiratory illness is severe enough to require intubation and mechanical ventilation. The case fatality among persons with illness meeting the current WHO case definition for probable and suspected cases of SARS is around 3%.

Chest radiographs may be normal during the febrile prodrome and throughout the course of illness. However, in a substantial proportion of patients, the respiratory phase is characterized by early focal infiltrates progressing to more generalized, patchy, interstitial infiltrates. Some chest radiographs from patients in the late stages of SARS have also shown areas of consolidation.

Early in the course of disease, the absolute lymphocyte count is often decreased. Overall white cell counts have generally been normal or decreased. At the peak of the respiratory illness, up to half of patients have leukopenia and thrombocytopenia or low-normal platelet counts (50,000–150,000/μl). Early in the respiratory phase, elevated creatine phosphokinase levels (up to 3000 IU/L) and hepatic transaminases (2- to 6-times the upper limits of normal) have been noted. Renal function has remained normal in the majority of patients.

Treatment regimens have included a variety of antibiotics to presumptively treat known bacterial agents of atypical pneumonia. In several locations, therapy has also included antiviral agents such as oseltamivir or ribavirin. Steroids have also been given orally or intravenously to patients in combination with ribavirin and other antimicrobials. At present, the most efficacious treatment regime, if any is unknown.

Airborne transmission—Spread by or through the air.

Antibacterial—Having the properties of an antibiotic; able to kill bacteria or suppres their growth and reproduction.

Antibiotic—A substance that destroys bacteria or suppresses their growth orreproduction.

Antibody—Blood protein that is produced in response to the presence of a foreign substance (such as a bacterium or virus) in the body.

Antiviral—Drugs that stimulate cellular defenses against viruses, reducing cell DNA synthesis and making cells more resistant to viral genes.

Asymptomatic—Showing no symptoms of a disease.

Atypical pneumonia—Pneumonia (a respiratory infection) that does not respond to penicillin, but does respond to such antibiotics as tetracycline and erythromycin.

Bronchoscopy—A medical procedure that allows the doctor to view the bronchi (small air sacs) of the lungs.

Capsid—Protein coat that surrounds a virus.

Case fatality rate—Number of fatalities from a specified disease in a given period of time.

Cluster—A group of cases of a disease, closely linked in time and place.

Communicable disease—A disease that is easily transmitted between people.

Coronavirus—Group of viruses that have a crown-like appearance and are responsible for most respiratory infections.

DNA (deoxyribonucleic acid)—The genetic material of nearly all living organisms, which controls heredity and is located in the cell nucleus.

Endotracheal intubation—A procedure where a tube is placed down the windpipe (trachea) to allow the patient to breathe.

Epidemic—A rapid increase in the numbers of cases of an infection.

Febrile—Having a fever.

Glossary

Genome—An organism's genetic material.

Germ theory—A theory which states that diseases are caused by microorganisms.

HCoV (human coronavirus)—A new coronavirus responsible for causing severe acute respiratory syndrome (SARS) in humans.

Host—A person or other living organism that can be infected by an infectious agent under natural conditions.

Immunomodulatory—Capable of modifying or regulating one or more immune functions.

Incidence—The rate at which new cases of infection arise in a population.

Incubation period—The time that elapses between infection and the appearance of symptoms of a disease.

Index patient—First patient to come down with a particular disease.

Infectious—Any disease that can be transmitted from one person to another.

Inoculum—A substance or organism that is introduced into surroundings suited to cell growth.

Isolation—The separation of persons who have a specific infectious illness from those who are healthy.

Leukopenia —An abnormal lowering of the blood white cell count.

Lymphopenia—Reduction in the number of lymphocytes (white blood cells).

Microorganism—An organism of a very small (microscopic) size.

Mortality—The per capita death rate in a population.

Nebulizer—A device used to deliver medicine directly to the lungs via an inhalable spray.

Nosocomial—Infection acquired in a hospital.

Oral-fecal transmission—The spread of the disease through the contamination of food with feces. This may occur when someone who has a disease does not wash his or her hands properly after using the bathroom, then prepares or otherwise touches food or utensils that another person puts into his or her mouth.

Outbreak—A sudden increase in the number of cases of a disease in a particular areas; an epidemic.

Pathogen—Any disease-producing microorganism.

Peplomers—Subunits of a virus particle.

Prevalence—The proportion of the host population infected at a given time.

Prophylactic—Preventative measure.

Quarantine—The enforced isolation or restriction of free movement of a patient to avoid the spread of a contagious disease.

Replicate—When DNA makes copies of itself as a cell divides.

RNA (ribonucleic acid)—Substance involved in the transmission of genetic information.

RT-PCR (reverse transcription–polymerase chain reaction)—A method for finding and determing the kind of mRNA (messenger RNA; a copy of genetic information from an organism's DNA) in a sample of cells from an organism.

Sputum induction—A process to remove sputum (mucus and other fluid) from the lungs.

Thrombocytopenia—An abnormally low number of thrombocytes (platelets).

Vaccine—Substance that triggers the production of antibodies that latch onto viruses. Vaccines also prompt white blood cells called macrophages to eat and destroy the antibody-tagged viruses.

Viral load—The amount of virus that is present in an infected person's bloodstream.

Glossary

Virulent—Easily able to overwhelm body immune defenses and cause disease.

Virus—A tiny microorganism that is capable of replication, but only when it is inside living cells.

Anand, Kanchan, John Ziebuhr, Parvesh Wadhwani, et al. "Coronavirus Main Proteinase Structure: Basis for Design of Anti-SARS Drugs." *Science* 300 (2003): 1763–1767.

The Bantam Medical Dictionary, 2nd ed. New York: Market House Books Ltd., 1996.

Bastur, S. V., et al. "SARS: A Local Public Health perspective." *Canadian Journal of Public Health* 95(1) (2004): 22–24.

Berkow, Robert, ed. "Viral Infections." *The Merck Manual of Medical Information Home Edition.* Whitehouse, NJ: Merck and Co., 1997.

CBS News. "In-depth: SARS." December 2003. Available online at *http://www.cbc.ca/news/background/sars/timeline.html.*

Centers for Disease Control and Prevention. "About CDC." Available online at *http://www.cdc.gov/aboutcdc.htm.*

———. "Clinical Guidance on the Identification and Evaluation of Possible SARS-CoV Disease among Persons Presenting with Community-Acquired Illness Version 2." (January 8, 2004). Available online at *http://www.cdc.gov/ncidod/sars/clinicalguidance.htm.*

———. "Division of Global Migration and Quarantine. History of Quarantine." Available online at *http://www.cdc.gov/ncidod/dq/history.htm.*

———. "Evaluation and Management of Patients Requiring Hospitalization." Available online at *http://www.cdc.gov/ncidod/sars/clinicalguidance 1.htm.*

———. "History of CDC." *Morbidity and Mortality Weekly Report* 45 (1996): 526–528.

———. "In the Absence of SARS-CoV Transmission Worldwide: Guidance for Surveillance, Clinical and Laboratory Evaluation, and Reporting Version 2." (January 21, 2004). Available online at *http://www.cdc.gov/ncidod/sars/absenceofsars.htm.*

———. "Preliminary Clinical Description of severe Acute Respiratory Syndrome." *Morbidity and Mortality Weekly Report* 52 (2003): 255–256. Available online at *http://www.cdc.gov/mmwr/preview/mmwrhtml/.*

Bibliography

———. "Public Health Guidance for Community-Level Preparedness and Response to Severe Acute Respiratory Syndrome (SARS) Version 2. Community-Based Control Measures." January 8, 2004. Available online at *http://www.cdc.gov/ncidod/sars/guidance/D/community.htm*.

———. "Public Health Guidance for Community-Level Preparedness and Response to Severe Acute Respiratory Syndrome (SARS) Version 2. Management of SARS Patients in Isolation." Available online at *http://www.cdc.gov/ncidod/sars/guidance/D/isolation.htm*.

———. "Public Health Guidance for Community-Level Preparedness and Response to Severe Acute Respiratory Syndrome (SARS) Version 2. Rationale and Goals. Center for Disease Control and Prevention." January 8, 2004. Available online at *http://www.cd.c.gov/ncidod/sars/guidance/D/rationale.htm*.

———. "Public Health Guidance for Community-Level Preparedness and Response to Severe Acute Respiratory Syndrome (SARS) Version 2. Summary." January 8, 2003. Available online at *http://www.cdc.gov/ncidod/sars/guidance/D/summary.htm*.

———. "Severe Acute Respiratory Syndrome." *Morbidity and Mortality Weekly Report* 2003–2004. Available online at *http://www.cdc.gov/mmwr/mguide_sars.html*.

———. "Severe Acute Respiratory Syndrome: Basic Information About SARS." January 13, 2004. Available online at *http://www.cdc.gov/ncidod/sars/factsheet.htm*.

———. "Severe Acute Respiratory Syndrome (SARS): Fact Sheet on Isolation and Quarantine." January 20, 2004. Available online at *http://www.cdc.gov/ncidod/sars/isolationquaratine.htm*.

———. "Threshold Determinants for the use of Community Containment Measures." Available online at *http://www.cdc.gov/ncidod/sars/guidance/D/apph.htm*.

Chan, P., et al. "Severe Acute Respiratory Syndrome-Associated Coronavirus Infection." *Emerging Infectious Diseases* 9(11) (2003): 1453–1454.

Cohen, Jon. "Do Clinical Masks Stop SARS?" *Slate* (April 2003). Available online at *http://slate.msn.com*.

Dye, Chris, and Nigel Gay. "Modeling the SARS Epidemic." *Science* 300 (2003): 1884–1885.

Guan, Y., B. J. Zheng, Y. Q. He, et al. "Isolation and Characterization of Viruses Related to the SARS Coronavirus from Animals in Southern China." *Science* 302 (2003): 276–278.

Holmes, Kathryn, and Luis Enjuanes. "The SARS Coronavirus: A Postgenomic Era." *Science* 300 (2003): 1377–1378.

Hsu, Ly, C. C. Lee, J. A. Green, et al. "Severe Acute Respiratory Syndrome (SARS) in Singapore: Clinical Features of Index Patients and Initial Contacts." *Emerging Infectious Diseases* 9 (2003): 713–717. Available online at *http://www.cdc.gov/ncidod/EID/vol0no6*.

Kamps, Bernd Sebastian, and Khristian Hoffmann, eds. *SARS Reference*, 3rd ed. Flying Publisher, 2003, pp. 1–172. Available online at *http://www .SARSreference.com*.

Lipsitch, Mar, Ted Cohen, Ben Cooper, et al. "Transmission Dynamics and Control of Severe Acute Respiratory Syndrome." *Science* 300 (2003): 1966–1970.

Lyons, A., and J. Petrucelli. *Medicine: An Illustrated History*. New York: Harry N. Abrams, Inc., 1987.

Maglen, Krista. "The First Line of Defense: British Quarantine and the Port Sanitary Authority in the Nineteenth Century." *Social History of Medicine* 15 (2000): 413–428.

Marra, Marco, Steve Jones, Caroline Astell, et al. "The Genome Sequence of the SARS-Associated Coronavirus." *Science* 300 (2003): 1399–1404.

Maybury, Bonnie A., and Pamela M. Peters. "Vaccines: How and Why?" Available online at *http://www.accessexcellence.org/AE/AEC/CC/ vaccines_how_why.html*.

Merson, Michael. "SARS Proved Health is Global Public Good." *YaleGlobal* 24 (September 2003). Available online at *http://yaleglobal.yale.edu/ display.article?id=2503*.

Ministry of Health and Long Term Care, Ontario. "SARS. Directive: Discharge of SARS Patients." Directive DS03-04. December 4, 2003.

Olsen, S., et al. "Transmission of the Severe Acute Respiratory Syndrome in Aircraft." *New England Journal of Medicine* 349(25) (2003): 2426–2422.

On-Line Medical Dictionary. Available online at *http://www.cancerweb .ncl.ac.uk/omd*.

Bibliography

Pang, X., et al. "Evaluation of Control Measures Implemented in the Severe Acute Respiratory Syndrome Outbreak in Beijing." *Journal of the American Medical Association* 290(24) (2003): 3215–3221.

Peiris, J. S., C. M. Chu, V. C. Cheng, et al. "Clinical Progression and Viral Load in a Community Outbreak of Coronavirus-Associated SARS Pneumonia: A Prospective Study." *Lancet* 361 (2003): 1767–1772. Available online at *http://image.thelancet.com/extras/03art347*.

Pottinger, Matt. "Megadoses of Steroids Devastated Many Chinese SARS Patients." *Wall Street Journal*, December 23, 2003. Available online at *http://www.sarswatch.org/comments.php*.

Ruan, Y. J., C. L. Wei, Al Ee, et al. "Comparative Full-Length Genome Sequence Analysis of 14 SARS Coronavirus Isolates and Common Mutations Associates with Putative Origins of Infection." *Lancet* 361 (2003): 1779–1785. Available online at *http://image.thelancet.com/extras/03art445*.

Sampathkumar, Priya, Zelalem Temesgen, Thomas Smith, et al. "SARS: Epidemiology, Clinical Presentation, Management, and Infection Control Measures." *Mayo Clinic Proceedings* 78 (2003): 882–890.

"SARS." *Mayo Clinic Proceedings* 78 (2003): 883.

University of Pittsburgh Medical Center. "Severe Acute Respiratory Syndrome (SARS): An Overview." Available online at *http://sars.upmc.con/Overview.htm*.

Veuzner, Gerhard. *500 Years of Medicine*. New York: Tapliger Publishing Co., 1972.

Wang, Chen G. "Research work on SARS has to be strengthened in China." *Chinese Medical Journal* 116(7) (2003): 963–964.

Wong, Janet. "SARS Outbreak Has University Impact." (March 31, 2003). Available online at *http://www.news.utoronto.ca/bin4/030331c.asp*.

World Health Organization. "Cumulative Number of Reported Probable Cases of Severe Respiratory Syndrome (SARS)." November 1, 2002–May 8, 2003. Available online at *http://www.who.int/csr/sarscountry/*.

———. Executive Board 113th Session. November 13, 2003. EB113/33.

———. "Global Search for SARS Vaccine Gains Momentum." November, 2, 2003. Available online at *http://www.who.int/mediacentre/releases/2003/pr83/en/*.

————. "SARS Epidemiology to Date." April, 11, 2003. Available online at *http://www.who.int/csr/sars/epi2003_04_11/en/.*

————. "Use of Laboratory Methods for SARS Diagnosis." Available online at *http://www.who.int/csr/sars/labmethods/en/.*

Wyngaarden, James B., and Lloyd H. Smith. "Viral Diseases." *Textbook of Medicine,* 15th ed. Philadelphia: W. B. Saunders Co., 1982.

Xin, Xiao. "First SARS vaccine tested." Available online at *http://www.china daily.com.cn/english/doc/200405/25/content_333679.htm.*

Further Reading

Abraham, Thomas. *Twenty-first Century Plague: The Story of SARS.* Baltimore: Johns Hopkins University Press, 2005.

Brookes, Timothy J. *Behind the Mask: How the World Survived SARS, the First Epidemic of the Twenty-first Century.* Washington, D.C.: American Public Health Association, 2005.

Chung Leung, Ping, and Eng Eong Ooi, eds. *SARS War: Combating the Disease in Singapore.* River Edge, NJ: World Scientific, 2003.

Goudsmit, Jaap. *Viral Fitness: The Next SARS and West Nile in the Making.* New York: Oxford University Press, 2004.

Kasper, Dennis L., Eugene Braunwald, Anthony Fauci, Stephen L. Hauser, and Dan L. Longo, eds. *Harrison's Principles of Internal Medicine,* 16th ed. New York: McGraw-Hill, 2004.

Loh, Christine. *At the Epicentre: Hong Kong and the SARS Outbreak.* Aberdeen, Hong Kong: Hong Kong University Press, 2004.

Websites

The Centers for Disease Control and Prevention
http://www.cdc.gov

Health Canada
http://www.hc-sc.gc.ca/

Medline Plus
http://medlineplus.gov/

The National Institutes of Health
http://www.nih.gov/

SARS Reference
http://www.sarsreference.com/

The World Health Organization
http://www.who.int

Index

AIDS, 7
Airborne transmission, 40, 97
Animal-to-human transmission, 35–36, 38–39, 54–55
Anthrax, 6, 65
Antibacterial (defined), 97
Antibiotics, 64–66, 97
Antibody, 49, 97
Antiviral (defined), 97
Antiviral drugs, 66
Asia, economic impact of SARS, 16, 83
Asymptomatic (defined), 97
Asymptomatic contacts, 23
Atypical pneumonia, 18, 97

Bangkok, Thailand, 11
B cells, 31
Beijing, China, 15
Blood tests, 55, 57
Body defenses against disease, 30–32
Bronchoalveolar lavage, 37
Bronchoscopy, 42, 97

Canada, 13, 14, 19, 44
Capsid, 28, 97
Case definition, 58–60
Case fatality rate, 23, 97
CDC factsheet, 92–94
Centers for Disease Control and Prevention (CDC) history of, 46, 75–76 response to epidemic, 41, 85, 93–94
Cheng, Johnny, 10–11, 19
Chicken cholera, 26
Children, 23

China
cover-up of initial outbreak, 19
initial SARS cases, 13, 15, 18–19, 35–36
travel precautions in, 82
vaccine development, 68–69
Chinese ferret badger, 38, 54
Cilia, as defense mechanism, 30
Civet, masked palm, 36, 38, 39, 54
Close contact, 42, 93
Cluster, 19, 97
Communicable disease, 40, 97
Community transmission, 54–55, 70–71, 72
Complex viruses, 32, 33
Confirmed case, 59
Control measures. See Public health control measures
Coronavirus (CoV) defined, 97
disease incidence, 35
infectious nature of, 16, 18
photomicrograph, 34
structure of, 32–35
Corticosteroids, 66–67
CoV. See Coronavirus
Cowpox, 70
Cryptosporidiosis, 6

Deaths from SARS, 17, 21, 23, 92
Defenses against disease, 30–32
de Freudenreich, E., 65
Diagnostic tests, 49, 50, 55–58, 59–61

Division of Global Migration and Quarantine, 46
DNA (deoxyribonucleic acid), 28, 97
Drug development, 7
Drug resistance, 6
Drugs for SARS, 64–67

Economic impact of SARS, 14, 16, 80–83
Elderly, 23, 50
Endotracheal intubation, 40, 97
Enveloped viruses, 32
Epidemic, 97. See also SARS outbreak (2003)
Epidemiology, in diagnosis, 49

Fatality rate, 23, 97
Febrile (defined), 97
Federal Quarantine Legislation, 46
Fleming, Alexander, 65

Genome
defined, 98
human, 7
SARS-CoV, 38–39
Germ theory of disease, 24–27, 65, 98
Global transportation. See International travel
Guangdong province, China, 15, 18, 35–36

Hantavirus, 6
HCoV (human coronavirus), 35, 98
Health-care workers, 10, 40–42, 45, 50–53

Helical viruses, 32, 33
Herbal remedies, 67
Home isolation, 72–74
Hong Kong, 10, 11, 13, 19
Hospitals, transmission
    in, 40–42, 43, 45,
    51–53, 74–75
Host (defined), 18, 98
Host interactions, 28–30
Human coronavirus
    (HCoV), 35, 98
Human genome, 7

Icosahedral viruses, 32,
    33
Immune system, as viral
    defense, 30–32
Immunity, 49
Immunoglobulins, 67
Immunomodulatory
    (defined), 98
Immunomodulatory
    therapy, 64, 66
Incidence, 35, 98
Incubation period, 50, 95,
    98
Index patient, 42, 98
Infection (defined), 24
Infectious (defined), 16,
    98
Infectious diseases, history
    of fight against, 6–7
Influenza vaccination, 76
Inoculum, 42, 98
Interferons, 67
International travel
    and disease transmis-
        sion, 6
    SARS outbreak and,
        14, 16, 80–83
Isolation, 23, 48, 62,
    72–74, 98. See also
    Quarantine

Jenner, Edward, 26, 70

Koch, Robert, 25, 27
Koch's Postulates, 27, 37

Leukopenia, 57, 98
Lymphocytes, 31
Lymphopenia, 55, 96, 98

Macrophages, 31
Malaria, 6, 7
Masked palm civet, 36,
    38, 39, 54
Media coverage, 83–85
Medications for SARS,
    64–67
Metropole Hotel, Hong
    Kong, 10, 11, 19
Microorganism, 24, 98
Mortality, 23, 98
Mucous membranes, as
    defense mechanism,
    30

Nebulizers, 43, 98
Nosocomial (defined), 98
Nosocomial infection, 43,
    45, 51–53, 74–75

Oral-fecal transmission,
    42, 99
Outbreak (defined), 99.
    See also SARS out-
    break (2003)

Pasteur, Louis, 25–26, 65
Pathogen, 99
Pebrine, 25–26
Peiris, Malik, 37
Penicillin antibiotics,
    65–66
Peplomers, 35, 99
Pneumonia, atypical, 18,
    97
Prevalence, 99
Prevention methods,
    51–55, 74–76

Probable case, 59
Prophylactic (defined),
    99
Protective clothing, 51, 52
Public health control
    measures
    in health-care facilities,
        74–75
    home prevention
        measures, 74
    isolation and quaran-
        tine, 23, 46–48,
        62–64, 72–74
    and public trust,
        77–79
    SARS epidemic and,
        85–86
    transmission preven-
        tion, 75–76
Public panic, 83–85
Public trust, in control
    measures, 77–79

Quarantine, 46–47,
    63–64, 99. See also
    Isolation
Quarantine stations, U.S.,
    46

Rabies vaccine, 26
Raccoon-dog, 38, 54
Replicate, 28, 99
Resistance to drugs, 6
Reverse transcription–
    polymerase chain
    reaction (RT-PCR),
    59, 99
Ribavirin, 66
Risk factors, 50–55
RNA (ribonucleic acid),
    28, 99
RT-PCR (reverse tran-
    scription–polymerase
    chain reaction), 59,
    99

Index

Salk polio vaccine, 75–76
SARS-CoV, 32
 genome, 38–39
 isolation of, 37–38, 57
 origin of, 35–36
 properties of, 35
 tests for, 59, 60–61
SARS outbreak (2003)
 cases and deaths, 17,
  21, 23, 92
 economic impact, 14,
  16, 80–83
 global spread of, 10–14,
  18–22, 92
 initial cases, 13, 15,
  18–19, 35–36
 media coverage, 83–85
 public health system
  and, 85–86
 response to, 23, 84–85,
  93–94
 timeline, 88–91
SARS (severe acute respi-
  ratory syndrome)
 case definition, 58–60
 causative agent, 14, 16,
  18. See also SARS-
  CoV
 CDC factsheet, 92–94
 control precautions,
  51–55, 74–76
 diagnosis, 45–46, 49,
  50, 55–58, 59–61
 disease progression, 50
 future directions, 86–87
 management of, 62–64
 risk factors, 50–55
 symptoms, 41, 43, 45,
  95–96
 transmission of, 40–45,
  92–93
 treatment, 50, 64–67, 96
 vaccine development,
  67–70

Singapore, 13, 19
Skin, as defense mecha-
  nism, 30
Smallpox, 6, 7, 21, 26,
  70
Sputum induction, 42,
  99
Sulfa drugs, 64
Superspreading, 45
Surgical masks, 53
Surveillance programs,
  72, 85
Suspected case, 59
Symptoms, 41, 43, 45,
  95–96

T cells, 31
Tests. See Diagnostic tests
Thailand, 11
Thrombocytopenia, 57,
  96, 99
Toronto, Canada, 13, 14,
  19, 44
Tourism, effect on, 14, 16,
  80–83
Transmission
 animal-to-human,
  35–36, 38–39,
  54–55
 in communities, 54–55,
  70–71, 72
 in hospitals, 40–42,
  43, 45, 51–53,
  74–75
 means of, 40–45,
  92–93
 prevention of, 51–55,
  74–76
Travel advisories (WHO),
  20, 22, 82
Travel, international. See
  International travel
Treatment, 50, 64–67,
  96

Urbani, Carlo, 11, 12

Vaccines
 defined, 99
 development steps, 68,
  69
 history of, 26, 70
 and immunity, 49
 for SARS, 67–70
Variolation, 70
Vietnam, 10, 11, 13, 19,
  85
Viral diseases, 14, 16–17,
  24–27
Viral load, 42, 99
Virulent (defined), 100
Viruses
 defenses against,
  30–32
 defined, 28, 100
 host interactions,
  28–30
 infection by, 30
 replication, 28, 99
 structure, 28, 29
 types of, 32, 33
Virus shedding, 60

World Health
  Organization (WHO),
  12
 global alert on SARS,
  20, 22
 mission of, 20
 names SARS virus, 37
 regional offices, 20–21
 response to epidemic,
  84–85
 summary of SARS
  cases, 17, 21
World Travel and
  Tourism Council, 83
World War II, 65